THE STORY
OF LIGHT
Volume 1
Path to Enlightenment

S. ROGER JOYEUX

Library and Archives Canada Cataloguing in Publication

Joyeux, S. Roger (Summermoon Roger), 1952-
    The Story of Light: Path to Enlightenment / S. Roger Joyeux;

Illustrator, Serah Roer. -- 3rd ed.

ISBN 978-0-9686521-5-2

1. Light—Religious aspects. 2. New Age movement. I. Title.

BP605.N48J68 2011   299'.93   C2011-902185-4

The Story of Light is a comprehensive and inspired body of knowledge about how divine light works on Earth and in the heavens.

www.thestoryoflight.com

This Book is dedicated to the trees.

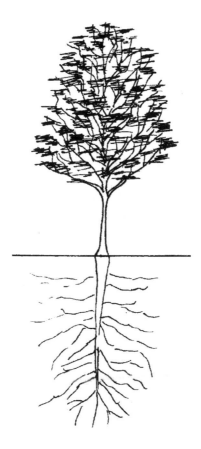

Their contribution to the enlightenment of Earth is so simple.
They reach into the sky to absorb the raw unprocessed light
frequencies of the Sun and then anchor them into the Earth
through their roots.

Table of Contents

Acknowledgements:

Thanks go to everyone who helped make this book possible—both the known and the unknown.

First and foremost, my guides the Councilate of the Ascended-Light are the original source for the material that is presented herein. Either they provided the material through channels sent to me directly, or they relayed information from other sources in the heavens. My good friend, Sarah Roer, was kind enough to come on board to provide the drawings that leave a wonderful feeling that the light is clear and uncomplicated. My wife, Judy, has been an inspiration at every step in the process of this edition. The book would not have happened without her. Finally, my thanks go out to everyone who purchased the first edition, and especially to those who offered their encouragements and who made helpful comments.

Introduction

This book is from the third printing of *The Story of Light, Path to Enlightenment*. There are a few changes from the original version to add clarity in places and to bring it up-to-date. Changes, however, are few, not many.

The spiritual path to enlightenment has speeded up in our current lifetime, but the principles upon which it is based have not changed. What has changed is the involvement and awakening of many newcomers to the spiritual path. Never before has there been so many individuals seeking the road to enlightenment and self-realization. When *The Story of Light* first came out in 2000, very few were ready to hear its message, and even fewer were ready to work with it. Since then, consciousness has risen significantly, and is now spreading like wild fire. I have always understood how valuable a resource *The Story of Light* is for the devotee who seeks to understand the spiritual journey and the way divine light works with us on Earth. To be entering a third version with rising demand for the book is the reflection of an ever rising consciousness.

Volume two, *The Story of Light, Through Heaven's Gate*, is now also available. Volume one is the foundation piece. I believe the reader would have a much more difficult time trying to understand how light works without having first become familiar with the many principles laid out in volume one. Although the discussions of light in both volumes are based upon principles that carry their threads throughout, there is almost no crossover of topics.

The Story of Light is a comprehensive and inspired body of knowledge about how divine light works on Earth and in the heavens. It was inspired from the heavens.

Over a period of a few years, I regularly sat in my meditation room and wrote four to five pages of material, dictated by a cadre of angels called the Councilate of the Ascended Light. To help with receiving the information, I have at home what I can best describe as a portal into higher consciousness. I refer to the copper energy bed mentioned in Chapter Two. By using the copper, along with crystals placed around me, I created a window between the third and higher dimensions. The window allowed the Councilate to plant a great deal of information into my conscious body. The information they gave me was profound. In the beginning, I was overwhelmed, intoxicated, and euphoric all-at-once. I was receiving the story of light.

The Councilate of the Ascended Light has served *The Story of Light* project by coordinating the flow of information. They are the directors. I am the incarnate channel and the writer. The Councilate is a cadre of some 36 angelic beings. All but two have, at some time, taken the incarnate form on Earth. As a group, the Councilate has participated previously in the evolution of Earth only once in the past. Shall I venture to say they were present during the activation of the Egyptian pyramids?

Their presence at this moment assists in the enlightenment of Earth and of individuals on Earth. Among other tasks, they work with the energy grid lines surrounding the planet. They are one of several angelic cadres that are creating linkages between places of light energy, wherever they exist on Earth, for the purposes of raising Earth's vibration and preparing it to receive its Light Body. The process of Light Body invocation, as it relates to individuals, is explained in Chapter Five.

The very first channels came to me in response to my curiosity about crystals. I had acquired a modest collection of various stones, but had no knowledge about how they worked. I asked the Councilate how I should use them. From the information given in the first few channels, I knew that I was being honoured with more than explanations about how crystals worked. The information went straight to how the light itself worked. Each channel revealed a small piece of a much larger puzzle, and each new channel built upon all the previous channels.

The information seemed vast, and it was. Each new idea added to material already received. A foundation of knowledge was built for me to share, and then expanded. Like the first bricks of a building under construction, the first channels foretold of the scale of the project, but did not reveal its shape or countenance. Without the first layer of bricks, the second layer had no place. Each piece of information supported the knowledge revealed in each subsequent piece.

This build-up of knowledge has been necessary because, without it, nothing made sense. The problems with light coming to Earth could not be understood without an understanding of the etheric body, first. The awakening of the spirit within the physical body (opening the Kundalini) could not be fully appreciated without explaining the development of the first chakra. The invocation of the Light Body could not be understood without prior knowledge of the role of love. All of the components of *The Story of Light* came in sequence according to divine intervention from my guides, the Councilate of the Ascended Light.

The records I received were not stored in one convenient location, complete with library file-cards giving the shelf number. At times, the Councilate gave me records they themselves held. At other times, my consciousness travelled to places so high that my Earthly memory could not possibly recall. As well, I know that I was visited by the keepers of some of the records directly. Sometimes, these beings accompanied my guides at the moment I wrote the channel to direct the flow of information coming off the end of my pen. Sometimes, they planted the record into my conscious body, as if to leave an essay for me to read later. A great number of the records were also received by channelling record-keeper crystals.

Records, held on record-keeper crystals, are denoted by a triangle configuration on the surface of the crystal's facets. The triangle carries the codes for an individual record and is the link to the Akashic Library, creation's ethereal storehouse of all memory and recorded experience. My own personal vibration carries its own set of codes that are the keys needed to open the Akashic vaults. Both the links through the crystals and the codes of my own vibration were necessary to enter past the keepers guarding the entrance to the records. When I used the crystals, my consciousness entered the Akashic Library.

From whatever source the records came, the complete record was downloaded and stored in my conscious body. Storage in my conscious body, however, is not the same as bringing the record into my mind's awareness. I was quite unaware of the vast amount of knowledge that I had been given. The original written channel was like the tip of an iceberg. Most of the information remained hidden within my conscious body.

Retrieving the hidden aspects of the records received was an easy, natural process. At first, without being aware of how the process worked, I merely set out to write the written channels. As I did so, a great deal more information surfaced in my mind's awareness to enhance the concepts at hand. In effect, each record was too large and overwhelming to be contained solely in the words of the original channel. I soon came to realize that my job included the incorporation of the hidden information into the text to provide the reader with optimum understanding.

Draft followed draft. In the beginning, I did my best to preserve the integrity of the channel as first offered. As the work of writing continued, I gained fluency in the language of the light. I began to think of my work with the material as my post-graduate study. At some point during this period of realization, my guides came to me in a very deliberate way. According to them, I had achieved mastery over the body of knowledge. They gave me licence to write as I saw fit.

My job has been to translate the concepts provided to me from the dimensions of the beyond, and even of the beyond-the-beyond, into comprehensible English. This translation did not come without a struggle. Sixth-dimensional wisdom for one, and eleventh-dimensional wisdom for another, were not created to fit into third-dimensional frames of reference, limited to width, height, and breadth and focussed only on the here and now. Nonetheless, with a little perseverance and much patience, *The Story of Light* found its way into written form. I am merely the translator of a body of wisdom destined to become available in our time.

The Story of Light approaches all topics on the basis of how they relate to light. This book is about light: it is not a "how to" or self-improvement book; it is not a personal story. It has depth.

The first and third chapters take on an historical context, and what you will find at their core are several primary concepts. Chapter One deals with physical density, and how it has affected the arrival of light on Earth. Chapter Three addresses the innovations that lead to the creation of the first chakra and the innovations from which the spiritual journey itself arose.

Chapter Two, "The Etheric Body", could not wait; it had to be placed as near to the beginning as possible. The etheric body's role in working with light is integral to almost every discussion that follows. Our personal identity, protection, vibrational stability, and everyday interaction with the world around us depend on the etheric body's ability to manipulate light frequencies. The section on etheric blue-printing generates its own interest around the topics of karma, birth, and astrology, but further, this section offers perspectives on how our spirit on Earth is shaped into the individual each of us has come to be.

Chapter Four discusses the seven major chakras. Each chakra was designed to make its own unique contribution to the process of enlightenment on Earth. Because this book is about light and light frequencies, it describes how the chakras work with light.

The final chapter, "Enlightenment", explains enlightenment. I have provided, what I hope are, clear definitions for the higher-self, the Light Body, and the soul, as a foundation upon which to explain the process of enlightenment. The time has arrived for all of us to clear away the clouds of mystery that surround spiritual growth, to tell the guarded secrets of the enlightened few, and to realize our potential as light beings. Enlightenment is a straightforward process that anyone having dedication, discipline, and love can achieve.

The Story of Light was built brick-by-brick. *The Story of Light, Path to Enlightenment* is the foundation for understanding divine light. Please allow me to present *The Story of Light, Path to Enlightenment*.

Love and light,
S. Roger Joyeux
www.thestoryoflight.com

Chapter 1: The Beginning of Light on Earth

1.1 The Will of God

Once upon a time, before time and life on Earth, all that existed was the centre of the universe. But there was no universe. There was no solar system, no planets, no Milky-Way galaxy, and no stars in the heavens. There were no heavens. All that existed was the centre surrounded by the void.

At the centre of the centre, at the very heart of all that was, is, and forever will be, is God. Yes God! God, Godhead, God-the-Father, Mother-Father-God, Allah, Shiva, the universe: each term is appropriate. Each term inspires the vision of the great creative force— God the all powerful—God the all mighty—God the creator. The concept of God transcends the boundaries of time and space. The vision of God is vast.

God created the universe, but creating the universe was not the first thing that happened. Creation and everything else depended upon God's will. Before God could be willing to create the universe, God had to be willing to be God. So, the first intention of the will of God was to take on the responsibility of being God. Having God first, and before the universe, brings logic to the start of creation. If God was to create the universe, there had to be a God first.

With God being God as God needed to be, all the rest began to unfold. God's first intention: to be God, was followed by his second intention: to create the universe. From God, the manifestation of creation issued forth.

In the beginning, God said: "Let there be light." God's will then drew upon the power of creation to extend outward into the void of nothingness. Creation issued forth in the image of God to be God beyond God. God projected from God to become the universe. So what happened was: God crossed the line. One minute he was all that was in the universe except that there was no universe; and the next minute he was beside himself, in himself, and everywhere else as well. God was both creator and creation.

Creation is an extension of God existing outside of the God centre. Think of it this way: the God centre always was and will be, and was therefore not created. Creation, on the other hand, arose from the will of God. As an extension outward from God, creation exists in the image of God outside the God centre.

God's will was to extend creation into every dimension. As the energies of the Godhead projected farther and farther outward into lower and lower dimensions, and into the void, its mass of vibrating light and form became more and more dense. The entry of creation into the third dimension heralded the beginning of the effort to bring the image of God onto the physical plane where vibration was slower and more dense than anything existing anywhere else in creation.

The living spirit of Earth stepped forward to volunteer to fulfill God's will for the third dimension. Every entity on Earth also stepped forward to fulfill God's will. Earth and its volunteers stepped into the void beyond God, beyond the light—to the very periphery of all that was. Earth took on the mantle of physical form in service to the will of God. Earth took its place in the divine plan at the most distant outpost in the universe.

The fulfilment of God's ancient goal for Earth follows the same pattern that was set down in numerous instances before. God extended outward as form, as planets and galaxies and stars, into dimensions farther and farther from the God centre. The formless aspect of God—spirit-light—then followed to join with form. Earth is the lowest level of manifest-form to be brought into the grace of divine illumination. Earth's turn has come. Earth will be enlightened. Because the will of God remains intact as originally expressed, the continuous flow of God's divine love, energies, and light will eventually lead to the realization of Earth's destiny of enlightened union with all of creation. The story of light begins with the will of God to extend the divine spirit-light into all created manifest-form, and now into the Earth fully and completely.

Our mission on Earth is to fulfill the will of God.

1.2 Light + Form = Oneness

God manifested as form, yet also exists without form. God is the galaxies and stars, the angels and planets, the Earth and Moon, the trees and grass, and the little boy climbing the tree. We know God when she expresses in form[1]. God needs form to be present in the world of creation. But without form, God exists in a state of formlessness that has no definition. In the formless state, God is the unseen illumination of her own spirit—the light. God, then, presents her own image in the two states of the form and the light.

The two states of God: the form and the light, separate when they leave the God centre to enter creation. Within the Godhead centre, the form and the light exist simultaneously. Each is both complete unto itself and united with the other. God is whole. But when God projects energy into the void to create the universe, her first impulse is to extend as form. People and planets and my computer are examples of form. In the second impulse, God sends out the unseen formless aspect of herself through what we have come to know as spirit or light or universal energy. God sends out light frequencies. Form and light are in union in the God centre, but separate as soon as they leave to enter creation.

Although separated as they enter creation, form and light are the two states of God, and therefore, most capable of working together

---

1 The expressions of form are limitless. On Earth, everything of substance is form: from the soil, to living organisms, to the air molecules. In the subtle realms, forms are expressed as essence of being, as well as, nodules of consciousness. The vast angelic vehicles of light constitute form. Form, then, may be understood as a separation from the formless. If the light of the Godhead is the formless, all of manifest creation is the form.

harmoniously. The light of God empowers the form of God. In the same way, if a computer, including monitor, processor, and printer, is used as an example to illustrate the form, the unseen electrical energy from the wall plug which operates the computer, can be used to illustrate the light. Using our physical eyes, we cannot see electrical current, nor can we see divine light. Electricity empowers the computer; light empowers form. The incarnate form on Earth, human or animal, is empowered by its soul's light.

God exists as form and light. At all levels of creation, spirit-light empowers form with life. When the soul brings the light of God into the form of God, i.e., the incarnate body, life is born.

Death demonstrates again the separation of form and light. When the switch to the computer is turned off, the computer ceases to function. When the spirit leaves the body at death, the body also ceases to function. God is body; God is spirit. On the one hand, a body without spirit is lifeless. On the other hand, a spirit without a body has no place to express itself. The expression of God depends upon the fragile union of light (spirit) and form (body).

On Earth, form and light must be joined to fulfill the potential for life, and the same is true for every other level of the universe as well. Manifest-form extends outward from the God centre and is followed by its empowering light frequencies. Closest to the God centre, form and light combine at once. Separation is hardly apparent. As the distance outward increases, so too does the separation. The union of form and light becomes more and more difficult in each lower dimension. At the farthest edge of the universe, on Earth, the union of light and form is more difficult than anywhere else.

The union of form and light produces "Oneness". The simplest way to understand Oneness is to refer to the equation: light + form = Oneness. In effect, Oneness is the union of the two aspects of God: the form and the formless. Oneness is not the formless (light), nor is it the form. The presence of light does not mean the presence of Oneness, nor does the presence of form. Oneness is the term for the product of the union.

Because Oneness is composed of the two aspects of God in

union, Oneness and God are one and the same. There is an obligation to refer to the Oneness as God. Oneness is God in the first person and is expressed as the "I AM" presence. The I AM presence of God dwells in the Oneness. Although distinction is possible between the God centre and creation, no distinction can be made between the Oneness and God. Oneness is God wherever it presents itself, and so, Oneness exists both inside the God centre and outside as part of creation.

Inside the God centre, light is Oneness and a part of God, and form is Oneness and a part of God. There is no need for light to unite with form nor for form to unite with light. Both light and form stand on their own, but each can also be in union with the other. Once light extends beyond the God centre into manifest creation, it becomes frequencies of light. Form beyond the God centre constitutes manifest creation and takes on vibratory density.

Outside the God centre, God is incomplete until light and form unite. God connects with light frequencies and connects with manifest form, but God cannot dwell in either alone as the I AM presence in the first person. Neither form without light, nor light without form, fully expresses the image of God, nor can either alone be Oneness. Outside the God centre, Oneness—God in the first person—is only possible when form and light are joined.

1.3 Black: The Light of Earth

Outside the divine God centre is the void, Oneness, form, and light frequencies. Although God is the essence of manifest-form and light, he dwells as the I AM presence only in the Oneness. In the void beyond the Oneness, God's creation has not yet arrived. The void is pristine nothingness.

Earth stepped boldly forward into the void to displace the nothingness with its divinely manifest form. Light followed Earth's form, yet crucial problems soon became apparent. Earth's form was unable to assimilate the light frequencies available because its physical vibration was too dense. Without light, Earth could not become Oneness. God's presence was not possible. A solution was needed.

Creation issues forth as manifest-form, light follows to combine with the form, and Oneness results. At every level of creation, manifest-form precedes the arrival of light. Similarly, the vibration, that has come to be the Earth, first extended into the void as form. Light followed. In the upper dimensions, combining form and light was easy and almost routine; few difficulties arose. On the Earth's lowly third dimension, however, combining divine light with physical form was an almost insurmountable challenge.

The problem on Earth was the need for light frequencies that could be assimilated into the very lowest and densest of manifest-forms. Nothing in the upper dimensions could have anticipated the extreme difficulty involved with fulfilling God's will to bring light into created form here on Earth. The very high and subtle frequencies of the higher dimensions were incompatible with dense physical form. Their assimilation was impossible.

The story of the first light to come to Earth begins with the slowest and densest light frequency of all—black light. Black is the Earth's indigenous light frequency.

Black light carries both negative and positive polarities, and is the lowest vibration of light on Earth. It is incapable of further densification. Black light resonates in the deepest levels[2] of the third dimension closer to the border with the void than any other frequency. Because Earth dwells at the very periphery of the void, black light

---

2 Today's world carries a very stable third-dimensional vibration, but this has not always been the case. Prior to the construction of the Egyptian pyramids, the third dimension vacillated substantially. Some third-dimensional vibrations vibrated at the high end of the vibrational scale and often shifted back and forth between the third and fourth dimensions. Other third-dimensional vibrations were at the low end and were extremely dense indeed. Anchored by the pyramids, a grid, encompassing the globe, was created by the ancient Egyptians to stabilize third-dimensional vibration. Consistency of vibration within the third dimension, as our world possesses today, was one of the contributions of the Giza pyramids.

was the most suitable frequency to initiate the process of Earth's enlightenment.

In the beginning, high and subtle light frequencies originating at the Godhead came directly to Earth along with black light frequencies. The vibration of Earth's form, however, was extremely slow and dense and only able to accommodate black light. Black light penetrated into Earth's space, while all other frequencies bounced off. But because black light assimilated with Earth's dense form, Oneness resulted. With Oneness, even in the minute quantities of those early times, came the presence of God in the first person—I AM.

Time passed. As the Earth attuned to the light of the black frequency band, Earth's Oneness expanded. Its vibration rose. As a result, other bands of light also became acceptable for assimilation to create Oneness. Form opened to marginally faster light frequencies one-at-a-time, but progress was extremely slow. During the first several millennia, the ability of form to accept light steadily improved. Each step in the evolutionary process resulted in the assimilation of a greater number of higher and more subtle frequencies. As more light entered form, more light was able to enter. The creation of Oneness from the union of light and form expanded, and so too, did the presence of God on Earth.

The enlightenment of Earth started with the assimilation of the black light frequency.

1.4 The Call

God's presence and her[3] expansion on Earth were in motion. God, however, was not happy with Earth's extremely slow progress. She issued a divine call for help throughout the universe. All beings

---

3 Throughout the text, odd-numbered sections (e.g., 1.1, 2.5, 3.3) express the masculine, and even-numbered sections (e.g., 2.2, 1.4, 4.6) express the feminine, wherever gender expression is required. In section 1.4, God's expansion is "her" expansion, yet if the same passage had appeared in section 1.3, it would have read "his" expansion.

of light and love from every part of creation were invited to serve in the enlightenment of the Earth and its third-dimensional vibration. Volunteers stepped forward. You and I, and all the other souls of the beings on Earth, volunteered to bring light where light had never been before.

Earth needed volunteers to take physical forms to work directly on the physical plane, and it also needed discarnate volunteers who did not take physical forms to serve from positions in the heavens. The angels stepped forward as both incarnate and discarnate beings to transmute the immense divine power of love from the highest places in creation directly onto the Earth.

Angels were easily recognized for their devotion and willingness to answer the call, but many other beings need recognition as well. The Earth's plant kingdom sent its legions, as did the animal kingdom. Through their roots and photosynthesis, plants anchor sunlight directly into the Earth. Every member of the animal kingdom is a receiving station for consciousness that radiates light wherever it goes. Fairies, elves, and gnomes, who live at a vibrational level just above the third dimension, came to serve the Earth as the cultivators of light. The nature spirits took on the important task of providing harmonic order to the cycles of life on Earth. Untold thousands of mineral formations arrived to serve as gateways for the direct transmission of light onto the physical plane. Each expression of creation that descended into the third dimension, consciously chose to answer the call. God's legions stepped forward as wilful volunteers in the greatest challenge of all—the enlightenment of Earth.

As the volunteers took on the mantle of third-level vibration, they became immersed in the extreme density of Earth. They were soon overwhelmed. Their ability to contribute to the divine will became encased in the limitations of physical vibration, and their consciousness on Earth slipped into profound dormancy. In truth, they fell asleep as soon as they arrived and lost all remembrance of their original purpose, as well as their connection with their higher selves. Their quest to fulfill God's will had to wait.

Millenniums of time would pass before Earth's vibration rose enough to accommodate the delicate light frequencies of consciousness needed to awaken the sleeping volunteers.

The problematic and slow beginning is also attributed to the Earth's will to receive light. During Earth's infancy, Earth was unable to focus energy wilfully. This meant that Earth was unable to generate the magnetic field patterns necessary to direct and stabilize the flow of incoming light. Frequencies scattered haphazardly. Light was lost. Consequently, growth and the expansion of Oneness were hardly noticeable.

The Call

Light coming to Earth was unable to move through the turbulent and dense magnetic field emanating from the planet's unstable form. Earth had yet to find the will to concentrate the flow of light effectively into the patterns that allowed assimilation.

Ultimately, the difficulty facing Earth's will arose from the same problem facing any being of light on the third dimension. The problem was a lack of knowledge. Light-beings from the higher dimensions had no body of wisdom to draw upon to obtain guidance. The third dimension was, as yet, an alien place. Although Earth willingly faced the challenges of the unknown, all that was known had to come from first-hand experience. Solving the Earth's problems meant living in the third dimension.

Do you remember answering the call?

The created universe began to unfold. You volunteered to serve the will of God by taking the ride to Earth. You braced yourself! Your ride ticket read,

God's Roller Coaster Company
Good for one ride, destination: Earth

Do you remember taking your place in line in the departure lounge of the Godhead? Do you remember thinking how brave you were to serve the will of God on Earth in the third dimension at the very edge of creation even before the beginning of time? The task did not appear to be all that complicated. How difficult could the enlightenment of Earth really be? Heaven was still heaven as far as the eye could see.

The roller coaster departed and your journey began. Moving outward from the Godhead, you encountered the upper heavens. As you held on tightly to your seat, creation passed before you faster and faster. Soon enough, the ride dipped steeply and accelerated. Everything became a blur. You rocketed past dimension after dimension, farther and farther from the Godhead. The rush offered no opportunity to appreciate the sights along the way. Creation was all around, but the light of the Godhead centre quickly fell behind. Darkness loomed ahead. Endless time went by. The light turned to darkness. You knew not where you were.

Thud!

Earth!

The roller coaster stopped, abruptly depositing you on Earth. The extreme density of physical vibration blocked your consciousness. Memory faded and disappeared. Where did you come from? What did you come to do? Did you pass through the heavens? Did you pass out of the upper dimensions? What are the upper dimensions? Are you the expression of creation? What is the lighted universe? What is the light? God? Who are you? You have just arrived on the third dimension. What is the third dimension?

The memory of who we truly are here on Earth has long been shrouded in the mists of time. What do we really know about how we came to be on Earth or why we are here? The unique and personal purpose each of us volunteered to fulfill is an irreplaceable piece in the grand design sent down from the heavens. We are an important part of the quest to fulfill God's will on Earth. We are here because we answered the call.

1.5 The Descent into Density

The volunteer beings who answered the call to serve were given responsibility for initiating the process of enlightenment on Earth. Their descent onto the physical plane brought them into hostile and unknown space at the farthest periphery of creation. Earth's destiny was to enter into the darkness of the void beyond the Oneness, beyond the lighted universe, beyond all that was known through experience. The Earth and its volunteers were the pioneers of the third dimension.

How did the heavenly hosts proceed as they stepped down from the dimensions of the beyond into third-dimensional reality?

First, and of great importance to the will of God, the decision to serve in the mission to enlighten the Earth was made freely. Each being, who answered the call, wilfully chose to come to Earth. At the level of our soul, each person on Earth has wilfully, consciously, and freely chosen to incarnate. Each is indeed responsible for his own presence here on Earth.

Once the descent into matter reached below the fourth dimension, the incarnate volunteers came upon the experience of time and space. Earthly time began with the rise of the Sun and the fall of the Moon. Day was born, then came night. As vibration drifted farther and farther away from the enlightened upper dimensions, it became immersed in the density of the physical plane.

The notion that all time and space is One, and in harmony and union, soon yielded to the problems of Earthly time and defined space. Time became linear; space became finite with clear boundaries. As past-time separated from future-time, the now-moment emerged.

11

All experiences on Earth occur strictly in the now-moment, not in the past or future. The separation of time was complemented by the separation of space. Because our Earthly consciousness cannot exist separate from "here", experience cannot take place in the separated space of "there". "Here" and "there" on Earth are not unified within the Oneness as they are in the heavens. Action, life, and awareness are only possible on Earth in the here and now. Reading these words only happens as an experience of the here-and-now.

The shock of moving from the eternity of time and the omnipresence of space in the heavens to the prison of Earth's here and now was beyond any preconceived expectation. Time and space took on the specific characteristics and limitations of the third dimension. This does not imply that the concepts of Earthly time and space were not already indigenous to the physical plane—they were indigenous. Rather, time and space were yet to be experienced in third-dimensional terms.

In addition to the limitations of time and space, Earth and its volunteers entered the duality of polar opposites. On one side was the positive-yang-masculine polarity, and on the other side was the negative-yin-feminine polarity. In the heavens, the opposing polarities within duality exist in mutual harmony and union immersed in Oneness. But on Earth, duality is defined by separation. Earth's volunteers could intellectually understand separation and duality, but they had come from the heavens. Their experience of Earthly separation and duality lay before them.

The first experience of duality came upon entering the Earth's physical plane. Earth's volunteers gravitated to one or the other side. Individual identity with the yin polarity or the yang polarity became dominant. Good guy versus bad guy, victim versus victimizer, police versus criminal, Christian versus heretic, and God versus the devil are simple examples of the separations within duality. Neither side is judged as desirable or undesirable. Both polarities, positive and negative, merely imply states of being that exist in opposition to each other. The most universal separation has been between the male and female sexes.

Adaptation of the volunteer light-workers to the physical plane was rife with difficulties. The trauma of densification into third-dimensional vibration generated profound memory loss. As a result, the incarnate light-workers forgot about their connection with the God source, as well as their union with all of creation as One. Earth presented the most hostile and foreign environment then imaginable. At the moment of entry, without any clear understanding of how to bring light to this lightless place, and without any knowledge of the third dimension's own peculiar characteristics, the task was beyond comprehension to both discarnate and incarnate beings. The separations of time, space, and dual polarities have presented some of the greatest challenges to life on Earth, but they have also provided the contrasts needed to expand our experience of physical reality.

1.6 The Pact of One

The descending volunteers soon grasped the difficulty before them. Fears arose as the descent gained momentum, especially upon entering the depths of third-dimensional darkness. Some beings easily integrated with the physical plane, but others mired in its density. Some retained their connections with the lighted universe and higher-self, while others were lost and condemned to wander the Earth. Realizing the problems that lay ahead, Earth's volunteer light-workers took the vow to be as One with each other again in the lighted realms.

The vow, or "Pact of One", arose from the love of Earth's volunteer light-workers for each other. They shared the perception, that the strength of those able to adapt to Earth to reach enlightenment and to achieve liberation from the cycle of birth-death-incarnation, was needed by those who were unable to adapt. Being strong meant the raising of the vibration of the physical body. Light-workers, who were able to raise their vibration sufficiently, gained the freedom to return to the heavens. According to the vow, the liberated ones were sworn to use their position in the heavens to help raise the vibration of those left behind. Incarnate beings, who were incapable of evolving upward through their own efforts, were to be offered assistance from those who had already ascended from Earth.

Each volunteer light-worker, who entered the third dimension, acceded to the Pact of One. Accordingly, whenever an individual ascended to the heavens, they were obliged to return to serve in the ascension of those remaining. From the Pact of One, arose the notion of the master and the student. The enlightened ones returned to become the teachers of love and light; the unenlightened ones, who so chose, became the students. Lamaseries, convents, monasteries, holy orders, and religions were created for the purpose of giving the students a pathway to liberation. No one was to be forgotten or left behind.

The Pact of One

The Pact of One is a bond of love. It is the foremost record in the plan laid down by those, who descended to the third dimension, and is held in the highest regard. Through the honour, love, and light given to Earth's volunteer light-workers from their ascended comrades, this ancient and sacred covenant has been maintained throughout time.

It is my pleasure, as author, to honour the principle of the Pact of One by presenting these words.

1.7 Earth's Volunteer Light-workers

With the descent to Earth behind them, the volunteers went to work. There was no understanding about the nature of the physical plane. There was no guidebook and certainly no tourist information office. Everything about the third dimension was foreign and unknown.

Some volunteer beings, such as those in the mineral realm, descended immediately into the Earth's mass. Others, such as those in the animal kingdom, had to wait until the planet was able to sustain higher life forms. Within the plant kingdom, the simplest forms or those with specific purpose made the descent first. Once plants were firmly established, the presence of animals became possible. Because the human species was a very high life-form, it waited a long time for the right conditions. The entry of each grouping or sub-grouping of volunteer beings or volunteer vibrations occurred in sequence according to divine timing and divine planning. But more crucially, entry occurred only when the Earth's physical vibration made it possible.

Not all volunteers chose to serve in the physical form. The Earth's cultivators—the fairies, gnomes, and elves—decided that their service was best accomplished from the vantage point of a vibrational level just above the third dimension. At the higher vibrational level, the cultivators work to direct light into places where it can be anchored. If a space, place, person, or thing is ready to receive light, the cultivators re-work and shape the light into acceptable frequencies. The next time you feel a tingle in your spine, it may be the cultivators opening your body to light.

Other volunteers chose to serve either in the incarnate form on Earth or the discarnate form in the heavens. Discarnate volunteer light-workers are the caretakers and managers of Earth's daily life. They reside in the lower heavens above the third dimension and are responsible for keeping the mission to fulfill God's will on-track. Angels are a prominent example. Many beings on Earth, and most of those reading these words, are incarnate angels. One of the

Earth's better known angelic cadres is the Great White Brotherhood of love , light, and learning whose members have worked with Earth and Earth's inhabitants since the beginning of the descent into matter. With every step in the Earth's long history, the Great White Brotherhood[4] has guided our evolutionary progress. Members of the Brotherhood are at work in both discarnate and incarnate forms.

The many difficulties behind the task of enlightening the Earth soon became apparent. Without knowing anything about physical vibration, service in the third dimension necessitated a great deal of creative innovation and experimentation. What is now known had to be learned. The wisdom of the Earth was accumulated solely through our collective experience as light-workers in physical form.

The first of Earth's volunteer beings, the mineral kingdom, took up residence as deposits randomly distributed throughout the planet. Because the minerals were among the first to arrive, their ability to assimilate light was crucial to Earth's early progress. In concert with the mineral kingdom, but from the vantage point of the heavens, the discarnate angelic caretakers of Earth made careful note of how minerals anchored light best. They measured the quantity and quality of light assimilated by specific minerals.

Learning about light on Earth was soon grounded in the practical approach and took on the appearance of the scientific experiment. The caretaker angels observed the vibrational rate of the planet at given moments in Earth time and calculated changes. Any change in vibration was greatly noticed. For a long period of time, the minerals were the only vibration capable of sustaining a presence in the third dimension. The contribution they made to Earth's overall vibration was felt with every frequency assimilated.

When light unites with minerals, Oneness expands. In turn, the expansion of the Oneness opens the door to bring a greater range of light frequencies onto the Earth. As the quantity and quality of

---

4 The Great White Brotherhood may also be called The Great White Brotherhood of Love, Light, and Learning. As it is an angelic cadre, it is inclusive of both genders without prejudice. The word "White" in their name indicates purity and white light.

light grows, so too, does the presence of the Oneness. By knowing which minerals held and assimilated light best, the caretaker angels knew which minerals, as well as which frequencies, to send to Earth. With each additional frequency assimilated, the Earth's minerals, rocks, and crystals fulfilled their service to the enlightenment process. Earth's vibrational rate rose very slightly every time a light frequency was assimilated into its mass. As Oneness expanded, evolution slowly gained speed.

Of all the Earth's minerals, the most capable of descending into physical form and of attracting and anchoring light is Obsidian. No other mineral assimilates light better. Although Obsidian is the most potent light anchor in the mineral world, others including Hematite, black onyx, and smoky quartz are also important. Each one contributes to the enlightenment of the Earth by drawing light into itself to create Oneness. The light they work with is black light.

Because minerals are very stable physical forms, the quality and quantity of light they brought to Earth was sufficiently consistent that it could be measured. Further, because of their stability, their light-carrying properties became the standard for measuring the light-carrying properties of other substances on the third dimension. The light, brought forth by the trees, flowers, raccoons, lichen, cats, dogs, and human beings, comes in differing quantities and qualities and vacillates as it flows onto the Earth. The stability of the minerals, however, allowed comparative measurements of the flow of light, and thereby, an understanding of the potential for progress through time.

By offering its mineral mass for service, Earth yielded its first contribution to the fulfilment of the will of God. The work on Earth was underway.

1.8 Problems Encountered in Anchoring Light

In the beginning, the lack of knowledge about the physical plane was universal. The guardian angels were only able to guide evolution once they had accumulated some amount of knowledge about physical vibration. Each experience yielded a piece to the grand puzzle. Eventually, the larger picture took shape. With every experience, problems that slowed the enlightenment process on Earth, emerged for examination.

One of the first problems to emerge involved the Earth's etheric body. The etheric body serves to protect the Earth by attracting and repelling light frequencies. It is a magnetic field that emanates from the Earth's mass and completely surrounds the planet. Its magnetic properties attract positive and repel negative vibrations. In essence, the etheric body is a filter for light and energy.

At any one moment, the etheric body's magnetic field selectively attracts and repels a set range of light frequencies. When the etheric field configuration shifts, so too does the range of frequencies attracted or repelled. Frequencies, assimilated into the planet's physical Oneness, generate a shift in overall vibration and an accompanying shift in the configuration of the etheric magnetic field. As more and more frequencies are assimilated, the Earth's Oneness and, thereby, its etheric field expand. The expansion of the etherics means an expansion of the range of frequencies that are attracted or repelled.

The problems caused by the etheric body arise from its limited capacity to attract light. At any one moment, the etheric field pattern precisely reflects the vibrational state of the Oneness from which it emanates. During the first few millennia of time, Earth's Oneness was made up of form and light that was very basic, slow, and dense. As a result, the quality of the frequencies attracted and repelled by the etherics was also basic, slow, and dense. The amount of light filtered by the etherics was also limited by these same characteristics. Only an insignificant amount of light from external sources was able to penetrate the etheric body's protective shield. The etheric body's inability to attract the higher quality light frequencies, or to allow an appreciable amount of light through to the planet's surface, impeded Earth's progress towards enlightenment.

The acute lack of light created a secondary problem. When light is not strong enough or abundant enough, the energy needed to empower the etheric body to repel unwanted negative vibrations is insufficient. The etheric body's energies must be equal to or greater than the energies of any invading negative vibrations for it to repel effectively. When light is in short supply, the etherics become weak. In its infancy, the Earth was vulnerable to negative energy because the amount of light needed to empower the etherics was inadequate.

To compensate for the shortfall and to protect itself, Earth wilfully concentrated the energy available to its etheric magnetic field. The concentrated configuration enhanced its ability to repel, but to be effective, the Earth's etheric body had to be very concentrated. Because unwanted negative energies and light frequencies were repelled by the etherics before they could penetrate into planetary space, the Earth was reasonably well protected.

The excessive concentration of the etheric magnetic field gave rise to the next problem. While filtering out undesirable negative energies, the etheric field also filtered out desirable light frequencies. Progress towards enlightenment, however, depended upon the availability of light. By filtering out desirable light frequencies, the evolutionary process was denied the light it needed. Minimal available light meant minimal progress which, in Earth's early moments, was unimaginably slow. Until the problem of etheric concentration could be alleviated, very little light of any kind became available for assimilation.

The shortage of light was compounded by yet another problem. When light arrived on the Earth's surface, it was absorbed by physical substances capable of grounding light—the minerals in particular. Some substances had significantly greater light-absorbing qualities than others. Unfortunately, the small quantity of light available to Earth was quickly lost to these dominant substances. Light-absorbing forms were unable to release light or make use of it in any meaningful way. In the early days on Earth, substances that absorbed light were not designed to use it. Without the ability to transform the acquired light frequencies into some viable use, frequencies were absorbed and stored, but remained grounded. Because they were unavailable, they were unable to contribute to the enlightenment process.

Etheric concentration, vulnerability to negativity, and the inability to use or release light were among the first problems to be encountered by Earth's pioneer light-workers. Numerous other problems loomed ahead.

1.9 Innovating Physical Duality

The problem of etheric magnetic field concentration was a serious impediment to Earth's enlightenment process. What to do? As necessity is the mother of invention, the angelic caretakers sought innovations that bypassed the etherics and facilitated the flow of light to the Earth. The physical plane's version of duality was one such innovation.

Earth's third-dimensional path was illuminated by the contrast provided by duality. Within the realm of duality, vibration was simplified into the two states of the black and white, the good and bad. It separated the yin, the female aspect, from the yang, the male aspect. By presenting vibration in one of the two polarities, and then generating its mirror image in the other opposing polarity, duality provides contrast. Through the contrast of opposites, the limits of physical reality became visible.

Whenever reference is made to the negative and positive aspects that make up duality, a third aspect found in the original state of any vibration has been left out. In the original state in the heavens, vibration involves a triad consisting of yin-yang-soul. The negative yin energy and the positive yang energy exist in union with the soul. Separation is absent. The soul, however, has been unable to enter the third dimension to anchor fully because it was neither acceptable to, nor compatible with physical vibration. Its subtle being-ness was too high to withstand the rough density and turmoil of third-dimensional existence. Therefore, the soul aspect has been withheld from Earth. Duality, then, involves the polar opposites of yin-yang, negative-positive without the presence of the soul.

Duality's contribution to Earth's enlightenment occurs when duality is surpassed by the reunion of the yin and yang. By combining the yin and the yang, the resulting construct is the original vibration or light frequency. Importantly, the reconstructed frequency acquired compatibility within the third dimension.

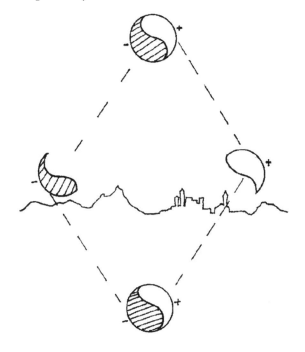

Light Splits to By-Pass the Etherics

In preparation for entry into the third dimension, vibrations of many varieties were split into their polar opposites. When a light frequency is split into the separate aspects of yin and yang, it loses its integrity. Neither the yin nor the yang aspect constitutes a complete light frequency in the true sense. The etheric magnetic field can detect, attract, and repel whole frequencies consisting of both polarities, but is ineffective when dealing with its parts. This meant that the individual yin and yang aspect was able to slip through the etherics unimpeded.

Each of the negative and positive aspects of a particular light frequency, that splits to come to Earth, continuously creates an attraction for the other aspect. Yin attracts yang; yang attracts yin. Once on Earth, their inherent polarity initiates their reunification process. Eventually, a light frequency's yin aspect combines with its yang aspect. Reunification takes place yielding a balanced light frequency that is whole, available, and useable on the third dimension.

To illustrate the process, picture the aircraft owner who folds up his aeroplane's wings, packs it into a crate, and then transports it to a distant place. Once at the destination, the aircraft is reassembled making it ready to fly. In a similar and humble way, the frequencies of divine light were transported onto the Earth through dismantling and separation into polar opposites. Separation allowed light frequencies to make the journey into physical vibration without being stopped by the protective etheric shield. Once on Earth, the separate aspects of yin and yang reunited through polar attraction to become as divine as they were before descending into third-level vibration.

Although the model of reunification is simple enough to understand, several problems hindered progress. Visualize a cardboard box full of different varieties of yin and yang particles floating and bouncing off the walls and each other. Also picture some particles entering and leaving the box in differing quantities and qualities. The problem: the yin and yang aspects were not always able to come together harmoniously.

But why?

First, although opposing polarities attract each other, they are often incompatible. The yin aspect of one light frequency may readily attract the yang aspect of another frequency, yet union can only occur when both are of the same frequency.

Second, union was frustrated whenever individual aspects became overwhelmed by the random jumble of disharmonious, dissimilar frequencies. An environment of turbulence, created by numerous incompatible and polarized aspects all moving in different directions, is not conducive to reunification.

Third, polar opposites move towards each other at varying rates and intensities and seldom come together in a balanced manner. Rather than merging harmoniously, they collide.

Fourth, both the yin and yang aspects can be of the same light frequency, yet one aspect may be more abundant than the other, thereby creating an imbalance. The excessive polar energy of the abundant aspect will be overwhelming to the less abundant aspect.

Fifth, because union occurs within manifest-form, the form is subjected to tensions caused by excess polar energy. If the integrity of the manifest-form's physical construct cannot withstand the tensions in polarity, it will disintegrate, and the energies accumulated therein will quickly dissipate. That is, within the context of the suggested visualization, the cardboard box itself can fall apart spilling its contents.

Incompatibility, disharmony, collision, imbalances, and the loss of form-integrity are a few of the problems that have slowed the process of reunification.

Turbulence and disharmony work against union; calm and serenity make it possible. Within a space of serenity, two polarized aspects of a light frequency are able to find the harmony needed to merge gently into a complete and viable light frequency. The propensity, to unite two polar opposites of the same frequency, has always depended upon their continuous attraction for each other. When there is an absence of turbulence, disharmony, and imbalance, natural attraction leads to union. Because of this principle and despite the difficulties, polar opposites did unite and whole manifest light frequencies were the result.

As an innovation for the purpose of bringing light onto the physical plane, the separation of the yin and yang polarities—duality—worked. Light, unable to bypass the etheric magnetic field, slipped through in a different and undetectable form.

1.10 Towards Enlightenment

Any being that can receive light frequencies into its manifest-form becomes Oneness to some degree. The presence of Oneness on Earth was established and began to grow with the arrival of light, first from the Godhead and then from the soul, upper heavens, and surrounding environment. Oneness implies the presence of God. Beings possessing Oneness also possess a measure of the powers of God, including the ability to create. Because God exists within, so too does the power to create. Light is created within. For any divine being anywhere in the universe, light comes from external sources, as well as from the Oneness within.

During Earth's earliest moments, light was in short supply. The high and subtle frequencies of the upper dimensions were not compatible with the dense physical plane, and therefore had to remain in the heavens. As well, the etheric body's energy levels were very low. The energies it did possess were used to repel undesirable frequencies, leaving almost no energy with which to attract desirable frequencies. Consequently, light available from external sources was extremely scarce.

On the other hand, light frequencies available from internal sources (within one's own being), depended upon the presence of Oneness (i.e., God), which in turn depended upon the prior union of light and form. Oneness created light, adding to the total amount of light on Earth. However, with very little light to join with form, Oneness was also in short supply. With almost no light from external sources, and almost no Oneness to create light from within, the planet's vibration appeared stationary for several millennia.

The process of evolution continued because a few frequencies did manage to get through. Although slowly, Oneness grew, and with it, the ability to create light from within our own third-dimensional physical beings also grew. Creating light frequencies from within does not depend upon anything except ourselves. Whenever the evolutionary journey on Earth stalled because light from external sources was unavailable, the light created from within maintained the process.

The light frequencies available to Earth were not always able to assimilate into form to become Oneness, but neither were they lost. A build-up of frequencies took place over time. Whenever light was assimilated by form, the union led to the expansion of Oneness. More Oneness meant more creative power, as well as, a rise in manifest form's overall vibration. Expanded Oneness also meant an expanded etheric body and a subsequent expansion of the quantity and quality of light frequencies attracted and assimilated. With an ever-increasing supply of light, progress towards enlightenment proceeded at a continuously accelerating rate.

During Earth's earliest moments, problems abounded. But with each problem, solutions were found. Light and form came together to create Oneness. Oneness brought the I AM presence of God and opened the way for more light to both come to Earth and be created from within. With each additional frequency, the vibrations of Earth and its inhabitants rose steadily one tiny increment at a time. The mission to fulfill God's will proceeded.

Chapter 2: The Etheric Body

2.1 The Etheric Magnetic Field

The etheric body, briefly mentioned in Chapter One, has a role in protecting the Earth. It is described as being a magnetic field that surrounded the planet and filtered light frequencies through attraction and repulsion. Because its presence throughout all of creation is pervasive, the etheric body is an important component in both creating the foundation piece of the story of light and the quest to fulfill our mission here on Earth.

Any object of vibration, including the planet, my pen, the human body, and the tree in the backyard has an etheric body that emanates an etheric magnetic field. Every vibration on the physical plane, as well as every vibration on every dimensional plane, emanates an etheric field. Your heart, liver, and kidneys each emanate their own etheric fields within the larger etheric magnetic field of the human body. A lake, a mountain, or a land mass has an etheric field. Every cell, molecule, and atom has an etheric field surrounding its form. The etheric body is essential to every manifestation of form created anywhere in the entire universe. Each planet is surrounded by an etheric field, as is every star, galaxy, and solar system. The etheric body emanates from and surrounds every part and sub-part of creation.

The etheric body projects outward from its source-form into a magnetic field that conforms to the form's vibration. It is neither object nor form, but magnetic, and possesses no vibration nor light of its own. The etheric body's magnetic field attracts light frequencies to its source-form to enhance the form's vibration and repels frequencies that endanger its form's stability.

The etheric field is comparable to a bar magnet with iron filings.

The filings reveal the patterns of the magnetic field as they form lines running to and from each magnetic pole in patterns that conform to the flow of the magnet's energies. The magnetic field of a bar magnet is a simple illustration of an etheric field. Instead of iron filings, the etheric magnetic field receives light frequencies also arranged according to the unique patterns of its field. If the flow of light can be observed, the etheric patterns will be revealed. Field configuration perfectly reflects the source-form from which it comes and changes simultaneously with even the slightest change in the form's vibration.

The etheric body is shaped according to the unique swirling, pulsing, and curving patterns of its magnetic charge. Light entering the etheric body follows the field patterns en route to its destination within form. In the case of complex organisms such as mammals, the overall etheric body is the umbrella for a number of lesser etheric fields. The etheric sub-fields of each organ, tissue, and muscle adds variations to an organism's etheric patterns. Each living cell also emits an etheric field that encompasses the tiny sub-fields of its component structures—the ribosomes, organelles, and DNA strands.

As light makes its way to the original site of attraction within the source-form, it must first journey through the vacillating magnetic fields and sub-fields of the etheric body. In the human etheric field, which is in essence the aura, the flow of light is strong enough to be visible to someone with clairvoyant abilities. Human and animal bodies are water-based. Therefore, light passing through a body is refracted into a rainbow of colours by the prism of water within the body's cells. Different parts of the body attract and refract different light frequencies. The colour that is visible to the clairvoyant is the dominant colour of the range of frequencies that are passing through a particular body part. Light passes into and out of the body through the etheric magnetic field creating swirling and vacillating patterns of colour. The patterns of the aura are determined by the patterns of the etheric field.

The auric pattern precisely reflects the bodily essence from which it emanates; and the colour of the pattern is exactly consistent with the vibration of the frequencies of that essence. Therefore, the presence of any tainted or diseased bodily form manifests itself as anomalies in the colours and flow patterns. Either the colours of the aura change or darken, or the flow patterns demonstrate dissynchrony. By assessing the flow of light through the human etheric field, a person's state of health can be diagnosed quite accurately.

All vibration, at any dimensional level, exists in a state of duality. All vibration, therefore, is subject to the attraction and repulsion of the dual polar energies within the etheric body. This is not to say that the etheric body of a piece of granite is going to have much influence over a flock of birds, or that putting a large bar magnet beside the Tower of Pisa is going to straighten it out. Each magnetic field has influence over a finite range of vibrations. For example, the iron filings of the bar magnet can be attracted, yet aluminum cannot. The etheric magnetic field works within a set range of frequencies consistent with the vibration of the source-form from which it emanates. Frequencies, that are consistent with the source-form, are attracted; frequencies that are not consistent are repelled.

If the light coming into the etheric body resonates harmoniously with the source-form's vibration, assimilation of the light into form takes place. The attraction for light, however, is based on magnetic polarity and not on resonant harmony. Light frequencies may be easily attracted by a form having a polar charge, but are not always appropriate to the form. The vast majority of frequencies attracted are not in resonant harmony and are not compatible, and therefore, cannot be assimilated. They are indeed disharmonious, but usually of no consequence, and simply pass out of the etheric field.

Although light flows through the etheric bodies of forms found in the heavens, as well as on Earth, significant differences exist. In the higher dimensions, the interface between light and form is extremely subtle. Light and form are totally immersed in Oneness. Form has its own individual identity, but is also unified with all of the rest of creation. The flowing motion of light into form is effortless. Light easily ebbs and flows through the etheric body with the rise and fall of wisps of consciously created thought-forms.

In contrast, the etheric body in the third dimension works with the very slow and dense vibrations of physical form. Light is either attracted or repelled. It does not flow with gracious subtlety. If the etheric body is weak, its ability to attract light will also be weak. It may not be strong enough to draw the needed frequencies to itself; and its repulsion of light may not provide adequate protection against the intrusion of unwanted frequencies. Even if the etheric body is strong, its attraction may include unwanted frequencies that are not fully compatible, and its ability to repel may adversely push away frequencies that are needed. Light on Earth, then, does not ebb and flow with the same ease as in the heavens. Whether in the dimensions of the heavens or on Earth, the etheric body helps manifest-form to harmonize with its environment.

The etheric body is a magnetic field that emanates from every type of vibration in creation. It attracts and repels and thus filters the light to which form is exposed. In the human experience, the etheric body's magnetic field establishes the patterns and colours for the aura. In addition to helping form to harmonize with its immediate environment, the etheric body can also help with form's harmonization in any dimension or between dimensions. Because all light must pass through the etheric body before it can be assimilated into form, its influence is profound.

2.2 Stabilizing the Expression of Creation

Creation arises out of the spontaneous pulse of the will of God. Each pulse yields a different outcome; each manifestation is unique. As creation issues forth from the Godhead, it takes on identity. In the heavens immediately outside the Godhead, created forms have identity, but are hardly distinguishable from each other. Created form, other created forms, and the Godhead are almost identical. However, subtle differences exist.

Form has its own defining features at every level of being. In the upper heavens, nearest to the Godhead, forms are so similar to other forms that they easily blend and merge. Energy flows as if boundaries do not exist. As distance from the Godhead increases, form takes on greater individual definition. Rather than blending or merging, form coexists with other forms. Separation between forms increases. By the time creation arrives in the lower heavens and on Earth, it is very defined. Third-dimensional form is the most defined outward expression of the image of God still capable of anchoring the light of consciousness.

In the quest to establish definition, the etheric body's magnetic field precisely reflects the vibration of the form from which it emanates. The vibration of each manifest-form is absolutely unique. Nowhere else in the entire universe is there another vibration exactly the same. Consequently, nowhere else is the etheric body the same either. When the etheric body goes to work, the range of frequencies attracted and repelled is directly contingent upon the state of its source-form's vibration.

Because the evolution and growth of form into Oneness depends upon the assimilation of one frequency after another in perfect sequence, the selected range of frequencies filtered by the etheric field determines the direction of form's development. High and subtle frequencies accelerate growth and lead to higher states of Oneness. Slow and dense frequencies mean slow growth and a retention of the basic states of Oneness. The etheric body regulates the development of its source-form precisely in accordance with the needs of the form's unique vibration.

The identity of a particular form, as distinguished from other forms, arises from the state of its vibration. In order to maintain its identity, form depends upon the etheric body. By attracting some and repelling other light frequencies, the etheric body preserves the vibrational state of its original source-form, and therefore, the continuity of its identity. With the assimilation of additional frequencies, the source-form's basic essence changes and evolves. Identity shifts very slightly as each change takes place.

Because the assimilation of light is rarely stable and constant, identity may also be unstable and may vacillate. If the bodily-form experiences a surge in the assimilation of light frequencies, change accelerates. If the surge is so great that the etheric body is overwhelmed, change becomes radical. The result can be a substantial shift in identity, with survival of the current identity coming into question. If the vibration and essence of form breaks down, identity is lost.

Losing identity need not be a negative experience. For example, a person who has chosen to be a break-and-enter thief emits an etheric magnetic field that attracts and repels the frequencies needed to stabilize her vibration as a criminal. Such a person is open to suggestions about quieter ways to break-in, how to fence stolen goods, and how to elude detection. If, on a given night, the break-in artist suddenly becomes a "born-again-Christian", change will be radical. The etheric field of the thief is quite different from the etheric field of the Christian. After turning a new leaf, the former thief is able to open to light frequencies consistent with Christ, such as respect, consideration, courtesy, honesty, and peace of mind among others. Because stealing and the newly assimilated light frequencies are incompatible, the reformed and now respectful, courteous, and honest person can no longer identify herself as a thief. Her identity as a criminal shrinks before the overwhelming light of Christ. So be it.

Identity and definition are of greater concern on the physical plane than in the heavens. In the heavens, vibration is totally surrounded by light and love and is fully merged as one with God. Any interaction between identifiable forms in the heavens is fully harmonious within the love vibration. Questions about the continuity of identity do not arise; and threats to identity are non-existent. On the physical plane, however, the interaction between manifest-forms and their environments is regulated by the etheric body. On Earth, love does not always rule; interaction between forms is not always harmonious; and assaults to identity from outside energy sources are real. The magnetic field of the etheric body maintains its form's integrity by overtly repelling offensive vibrations that threaten the survival or continuity of identity. On Earth, ensuring the longevity of identity depends upon erecting barriers such as the protective shield of the etheric body.

The etheric body serves creation by maintaining and stabilizing the qualities of its source-form's identity and by isolating its form from other forms, vibrations, and light frequencies.

2.3 Variations in the Etheric Field

The etheric body protects and maintains the integrity of its source-form, but does so within a changing external environment that can be both friendly and hostile. In the face of environmental variation, the etheric body experiences anomalies within its magnetic field patterns. Field-pattern anomalies are usually insignificant, yet they cause changes to the flow of light frequencies attracted and repelled and, therefore, to the process of enlightenment.

2.3.1 Cause and Effect

The etheric body stabilizes its source-form as best it can, yet every time the form changes, so too, does the etheric body. When form assimilates even a single insignificant light frequency, its vibration shifts very subtly, causing a simultaneous and equally subtle shift in the configuration of the etheric magnetic field. Subtle or not, the assimilation of light affects the vibration of the source-form, which affects the etheric field, which affects the assimilation of light, which consequently affects the vibration of the source-form, the etheric field, and the further assimilation of light.

Human growth and evolution follow a similar pattern. Using the intellect to illustrate, each fact, principle, or concept that a person's mind can grasp, reading this text for example, acts in the same way as a light frequency. When an individual acquires facts, principles, and concepts, he builds a foundation of knowledge. The larger his foundation of knowledge, the more learned he becomes.

Understanding facts, principles, and concepts is similar to assimilating light frequencies. More facts, principles, and concepts mean higher knowledge. More light frequencies mean form becomes a higher vibration. As higher vibration, it can then open to assimilate a wider range of light frequencies. Because changes to form's vibration are simultaneously reflected as changes in the etherics, the etherics also open to attract and repel wider ranges of frequencies. The intellect grows with the assimilation of facts, principles, and concepts; and the vibration of form grows with the assimilation of light frequencies.

The assimilation of light leads to changes within the etherics, but, so too, do many external influences. Understanding the relationship between the etheric body and the source-form, from which it arises, is an important step prior to answering the question: how do external influences affect the etheric body?

Affecting the source-form changes the etherics directly; affecting the etherics changes the form indirectly. In the first instance, the etheric field always emanates from its source-form. When the vibration of its form changes, the etheric field reflects the change immediately. In the second instance, changes in the etherics may or may not result in changes to its source-form. Changes to the form arise from the assimilation or release of light and not from changes in the etherics. But because the etheric body directly influences the quantity and quality of light it brings into its source-form's space, it facilitates change. If the source-form assimilates the light brought forth, its vibration will change. The etherics contribute to changes in its source-form indirectly by influencing the availability of light. Changing the form changes the etherics; changing the etherics is only likely to change the form.

Because the etheric body is magnetic, it is subjected to the influences of other magnetic fields. For example, the Earth exerts a magnetic deviation from the true north pole along longitudinal grid lines. All persons living on the demarcation of a particular polar deviation will experience the same magnetic influence. If, however, a person travels to a different place where the deviation is different, the influence exerted will also be different. Magnetic deviation is one example of an external influence that affects the etheric body.

How many magnetic influences do we encounter in a day? When a person walks close to a municipal electric utility substation, the electrical magnetic energy of the local area affects the configuration of the person's etheric field to some degree. The electrical wires supplying homes with power, the electric toaster, the microwave, the television, electric blankets, electric razors, curling irons, the garage door remote control, the magnets in stereo speakers, and cellular phones, are examples of objects that project magnetic fields that interact with our own etheric magnetic field causing it to shift.

Each environment that a person enters has its own unique vibration and subsequent magnetic influence. If the environment is positive, it will interact with the person's etheric field in a healthy manner and light for growth will be acquired. In contrast, a negative space will emanate an etheric magnetic field that will interact dis-harmoniously. The negative influence is likely to increase the density of vibration and may cause higher light frequencies to leak from the person's form. Whether significant or insignificant, almost everything a person encounters as they walk about the Earth has an influence one way or another upon the etheric body's magnetic field.

External influences on the etherics are not necessarily harmful or something to fear. Each influence is different and simply interacts with the etheric body causing some modification to the etheric magnetic field pattern. The pattern may or may not bend, twist, concentrate, or become contorted in some way. In contrast, the influence can also cause the etheric pattern to be brought into greater alignment with its source-form. Greater alignment ensures a more desirable flow of light. The change in the etherics caused by a pop-up toaster, for example, is unlikely to have any significant affect one way or another. The exact influence is very difficult to measure or to qualify, but every change in the configuration of the etheric field causes a subsequent change in the range of frequencies attracted and repelled to or from the source-form.

External influences can affect the etherics without affecting the source-form. For instance, external magnetic fields cause temporary shifts in etheric energy balance that can lead to changes in the configuration of the etheric field. Influences on the source-form of the etherics, however, come not from the etherics but from the assimilation or leakage outward of light frequencies. If the quantity and quality of light passing through the etherics remain unchanged, the source-form will be unaffected by the influence imposed upon the etheric body.

Although a shift in the etheric magnetic field pattern does not directly cause a corresponding shift to the vibration of its source-form, form can be seriously affected. When influences upon the etheric body cause temporary imbalances in etheric energies, the etheric field shifts away from its natural alignment with its source-form. The etheric body's connection with its source-form loosens. The induced imbalance can lead to holes, gaps, thin spots, dense spots, or blockages within the etheric field. The field can lose its ability to effectively attract and repel an appropriate range of light frequencies.

The incarnate individual's evolution depends upon the continuous flow of ever higher and more subtle light frequencies. Any disruption denies the necessary frequencies and has the potential to retard, or reverse, the individual's evolution. If the etheric body experiences further imbalances, frequencies that are neither harmonious nor aligned with the source-form will penetrate form's essence. Form's vibration may lose its integrity and stability, and its very survival may come into question.

Where does a threat to survival enter the etheric field?

A threatening or negative energy can vibrate at a frequency rate that is in harmony with the etheric magnetic field emanating from a vulnerable part of the physical body. Have your co-workers stabbed you in the back? Has your business competition been cutting you off at the knees? Did your lover break your heart? Although figurative, the examples have a literal implication. If the body part in-question is weak, its etheric magnetic field leaves an opening through which negative energy might penetrate into the physical form.

A weak physical body part cannot provide the etheric field with sufficient energy to do its job. Desirable frequencies are not attracted and undesirable frequencies are not repelled adequately. The consequence of weakened etherics is lower vibration. When vibration becomes too low, physical disease symptoms will manifest.

We live within an environment full of vacillating etheric magnetic energy fields that continuously affect our own etheric body. Any external energy that affects the etheric body causes changes to the flow of light to which we are exposed. Changes may or may not be significant, and may or may not be positive or negative. When the light we work with changes, so too, does our vibration.

2.3.2 Mindful Change

Because we humans exist on a planet of free-will, desires and choices account for much of the way we are. When we exercise free-will, we bring our conscious mind forward to influence our vibration and, in turn, our etheric body. The conscious mind is very capable of rearranging the configuration of our being-ness and subsequent vibration simply by changing. Changing the mind can be as subtle as deciding to purchase a green toothbrush instead of a red one, or as profound as making a pilgrimage to Mecca.

The mind articulates the flow of light within the human being's consciousness. It is responsible for creating conceptual thought patterns and for directing the activities of daily living. Whenever the mind is at work, scores of light frequencies are moved about within our bodies, thus altering the basic vibration of the human body's form. When the body's vibration changes, so does the etheric field. Moving light and changing the etherics inevitably results in the assimilation of new and different frequencies and the release of old ones. Moving light and changing the etherics also results in changes to bodily form and its subsequent etheric magnetic field.

Because the mind is inspired by the free-will from within, our own choices make a great deal of difference to the range of the light frequencies we encounter. If we choose to be joyful, the frequencies of joy are attracted. If we choose to be grumpy, we attract environments filled with discontent. As always, a shift in frequencies changes the basic vibration of our state of being and, thereby, the magnetic configuration of the etheric body. In effect, we can change our vibration by using the mind to make conscious wilful choices. The resulting etheric field does its best to attract and repel light frequencies that conform to our choices.

Because the mind has the power to manipulate light and reconfigure the etheric field to suit itself, change happens when a person makes up his mind.

2.3.3 Energy Conductors

The etheric magnetic field can be manipulated by external influences that impose their own magnetic energy, but it can also be influenced by a medium that does not impose magnetic energy. The influence of such a medium springs from the medium's ability to lower the resistance to the flow of energy already within the source-form's etheric magnetic field. Lowering the resistance accelerates the field, which is then better able both to align with its source-form, and to accomplish its task of filtering light.

Mediums that reduce resistance to the flow of energy within a magnetic field are energy conductors. They do not use their own energy or impose or displace energy to influence the existing etheric field patterns. Rather than projecting energy into the etheric body, the medium conducts the source-form's own magnetic energy. The true energy conductor accelerates the flow of existing energy without adding or subtracting its own energy.

Accelerating the existing energy of a person's body can have a profound affect on the body's ability to plug holes in the etheric field, to reinforce thin spots, to accelerate dense spots, and to clear blockages, imbalances, and weak points previously mentioned (section 2.3.a). When the influence of an energy conductor is applied, the balancing of energies begins immediately. Blockages are destroyed or dissipate; holes in the etherics disappear. Most notably, the energies of an accelerated etheric body will re-configure into the patterns of its natural state. The etheric body then comes into balance in synchrony and harmony and in perfect alignment with its source-form.

Balancing the etherics has a positive side-effect. Once the etherics are balanced, etheric energies, which are needed to keep the tensions of imbalance in place, are released. Released energies can then be used as they were intended: to vitalize the etheric body's capacity to attract or repel light with all power and strength. Attracting more light strengthens the vibration of the manifest-form, and in turn, strengthens its ability to attract even more light. Repelling unwanted light maintains the survival of form by removing threats to its integrity. An etheric body in balance uses energy appropriately. It does not need to compensate for the tensions of imbalance.

Conductive mediums that work well with the etheric body include copper, silk, gold, and silver. Silk is a natural product of a living organism. Copper, gold, and silver are atomic elements.

In contrast, metal alloys and compounds, may be excellent conductors, but are inherently made up of several different substances. Because each substance within a compound vibrates at a rate different from each of the other substances, conductivity is variable. When a compound is used to influence the etheric body, each of its components conducts a different area of the etherics at a different rate, thus creating a variety of influences within the same etheric field. The differing rates of conductivity work against bringing the etheric body into natural alignment with its source-form. Alloys and compounds tend to create more chaos than harmony.

Acceleration of the etheric field needs to be uniform to maintain synchrony and harmony. Because copper (as well as gold and silver) is an atomic element having its own unique and singular acceleration rate, it offers an even and consistent influence to the etheric field. Silk cloth also offers an even and consistent influence. Although silk's composition includes numerous substances, silk originates as an organic substance created by a living organism in harmony. Silk is spun from the living being of the silk worm and comes to Earth as living material, living threads of cloth. Copper and silk are the energy conductors of choice to accelerate and align the human etheric body. Gold and silver are more proficient energy conductors than copper, but price is likely to be prohibitive.

During the twentieth century, the use of conductive mediums to influence the etheric body began with bio-circuits and evolved to include the revival of some very ancient practices.

In the 1930s, bio-circuits were used as a healing device and studied extensively by Leon Eeman in the UK. They reduce resistance to the flow of energy in the hands, feet, and spine. To create a bio-circuit, a copper plate is placed at each hand with a copper wire connecting another copper plate placed at each opposite foot. Plates and a connecting wire are also used to connect the top and bottom of the spine. The wires and plates are direct physical links, that provide mediums through which the body's energy could flow. The bio-circuit was intended to aid the conduct of energies that build up in the hands, feet, and spine, thereby reducing tension and effecting balance.

With the rise of new-age spirituality, many light-workers have awakened to long-lost memories of ancient practices that used the tools of light. Memories, along with the guidance of discarnate light-workers such as the angels, fairies, and gnomes, have triggered the creative use of copper. Crystals wrapped in copper, copper energy beds to lie on, copper pyramids for healing and meditation, and copper wrist bands for healing and energy revitalization are a few of the uses common in today's world. Each application accelerates the conductivity of body energy by reducing flow resistance within the etheric magnetic field.

The copper energy bed, or copperboard, is a very practical way to bring the etheric magnetic flow patterns into natural alignment with the body. To make a copper energy bed, cut a sheet of 0.223 gauge roofing copper to a size of 7' x 3' and mount it onto a piece of plywood with epoxy glue. If a person were to lie on the copper for 20-25 minutes, his entire etheric magnetic field would be accelerated enough to assume its own natural flow patterns. Energy is not merely transferred from one area to another as it is by the bio-circuit. It is accelerated throughout the physical body's etheric magnetic field. The health benefits, for a person whose etheric field is vitalized, balanced, and naturally aligned with the body, are potentially significant. Using a copper energy bed will change your life[1].

1 Besides the primary task of balancing the etheric magnetic field,

Lying on a sheet of pure silk has the same basic effect as the copper energy bed. Both can be used at the same time without creating dis-synchronous acceleration rates. Although copper and silk each work with the full range of etheric vibration, copper works more directly with the lower ranges, while silk works with the upper ranges. By lying on either copper or silk, acceleration of the physical body's etheric field re-balances and redistributes its magnetic energies, and thereby, eliminates blockages and weak points[2].

Many compounds and substances act as energy conductors, but energy conductors, appropriate for use with the etheric body, include copper, silk, gold, and silver. Energy conductors reduce resistance to the flow of energy within the etheric magnetic field without adding or removing their own energy. Their influence is quite positive. They balance the etheric field, enhance the field's energies, and align the etheric body with its source-form, thus helping the etherics to work better at its job of filtering light.

2.3.4 Stability in the Face of Change

The practical purpose of the etheric body is to maintain the integrity, stability, and identity of its source-form. Change, however, is

---

the copperboard can work miracles with the common cold. I have been successful in reversing the onset of the common cold numerous times. A cold is usually noticeable after about a day or so. At that point, do one session immediately, then a second session later in the day. Do two more sessions the next day. By the end of the third session, the symptoms of the cold should be receding noticeably. By the end of the fourth session, the cold should be in full retreat. A further two sessions over the next two days should see the cold disappear.

2 As any substance within an individual's etheric magnetic field has some influence on the field's patterns, the individual lying on the copper energy bed benefits best without clothes or with 100% natural fabric clothing. Any other influences, such as synthetic underwear, jewellery, or metal zippers, create a disturbance in the natural flow patterns of the etheric field.

inevitable. Changes to the etheric body's source-form occur continuously; and the etheric body changes simultaneously and in perfect alignment. When the source-form changes, the etherics adjust to attract and repel the exact range of frequencies needed to maintain the form's changed vibration.

The manipulation of the etheric magnetic field, by other etheric fields or mediums, changes the flow of light available to the source-form. Outside influences, however, are not always detrimental. Some influences create imbalances in the etherics that actually facilitate the flow of light and enhance progress towards enlightenment. Although outside influences interfere with the attraction and repulsion of light, the results need not be cause for alarm.

Predetermining the consequence and consistency of the smorgasbord of influences that continuously surround a particular source-form is difficult. As long as the etheric body is reasonably well empowered and well aligned with its source-form, it will provide the stability needed to maintain the source-form's current vibration and identity against the imposition of external influences.

2.4 The Protective Function

The etheric body ensures that its source-form's vibration grows by attracting only compatible frequencies and by repelling incompatible frequencies. The protective function of the etheric body depends upon the etheric magnetic field's ability to attract and repel light frequencies within a set range that is consistent with its source-form.

Attracting desirable light is as integral to the protective function as repelling undesirable light. If the state of vibration of a manifest-form is weak, it cannot generate an etheric magnetic field with sufficient strength to repel all of the problem energies with which it coexists. Weak form is vulnerable. But through the attraction of light, the etheric body enhances and strengthens the vibration of its source-form. First, the form assimilates the light attracted into its essence, and then it radiates a stronger etheric magnetic field. In turn, the stronger etheric field can more effectively attract and repel light. The attraction of light provides the source-form with the vitality it needs to emit an etheric body capable of doing its job. By repelling negative energy, the etheric body maintains its source-form's integrity.

Negative energy can potentially disrupt the identity and vibrational state of manifest-form. A weak etheric body will have holes or weak areas through which negative energy is able to penetrate. If intrusion occurs, the vibration of the source-form is threatened[3]. The form's energies drain away; imbalances occur. As well, the identity of the form may change for the worse or even experience destruction. By contracting the size and scope of its magnetic field and by concentrating its energy, the etheric body presents a barrier to excessive or unwanted vibration.

The etheric body concentrates its etheric field to resist the intrusion of unwanted vibration by apportioning the quantity and quality of energy needed to be effective. If the problem is minor, concentration of the etheric field occurs at a superficial level. As negative energy penetrates into deeper levels, the etheric body's energy becomes increasingly concentrated. If negativity penetrates to the core to threaten survival, concentration of the etherics may consume all available energy. The etheric field assumes its maximum concentration.

To illustrate, severely abused individuals often have difficulty opening their hearts to others to develop intimacy. Their need to protect themselves runs deep. The degree of concentration of the etheric field around an abused individual's heart is proportional to the severity of the abuse.

How might etheric concentration apply to daily life? Here is an example scenario.

Johnny conducted his daily life in a quiet house on a street that could be found anywhere. Life was peaceful and generally worry-free.

---

3 Most delusions of grandeur among mentally-challenged individuals can be attributed to the intrusion of negative psychic energy in cases where the etheric field is weak or full of holes.

Johnny spoke to his neighbours once-in-a-while, but he was usually alone. He had only himself to be concerned about, with no need to close himself off from possible threats to his well-being. Because he was at peace, his etheric magnetic field was radiant and wide open.

Then Johnny's sister, brother-in-law, and their three children came to visit. His sister was critical of Johnny's housekeeping. His brother-in-law wanted to borrow Johnny's tools and car; he wanted to be the barbecue supervisor. The three children jumped on the furniture, broke two lamps, and made a mess of his newly planted lawn.

Johnny's relatives had invaded his personal space and turned his peaceful life upside-down. They had brought with them a significant amount of negative energy, against which Johnny was forced to defend himself. Johnny's heart had to close, but so too, did his etheric body. His etherics contracted to a fraction of its usual size, as it severely concentrated its energies. Before his etheric body could open again, Johnny would have to regain the peace he had previously enjoyed.

Johnny's sister and her family finally departed.

Disharmonious, negative, or disruptive vibrations cause the etherics to concentrate in defence. When these energies are removed, as they were when Johnny's relatives departed, the etheric magnetic field is again able to open. Protection is unnecessary once the bombardment of unwanted energy stops. The etheric field is then free to relax, or rather, to move out of its concentrated state. It thins out and occupies wider space.

Unfortunately, the shift from a concentrated etheric magnetic field to an expanded field does not often occur immediately upon removal of the negative influence. Etheric energies tend to remain fixed in their existing patterns. Until either their source-form's vibration changes, or the etheric field is subjected to further external influences, the etheric body's pattern remains. Demand for etheric energies elsewhere in the body is insufficient to generate the shift to a new field pattern. Inertia further contributes to the etheric body's fixed state. The creation of a new configuration of the etheric field itself takes energy, which may not be readily available. Until the energy available for initiating change is adequate, inertia prevents changes to the etheric body's magnetic field patterns. The concentrated etheric field can therefore remain fixed for some time after problems have been alleviated.

Because an element of conscious control exists, the concentrated state of the etherics often involves an incarnate individual's will power. In the face of threats, the conscious will sets its vibration (and thereby, its etheric field) into a defensive mode.

Negative energies may be immediate and real causing an almost automatic wilful concentration of the etheric energy field, but they can also be perceived. An individual's mere perception of a negative threat is as effective as a real threat. Both will galvanize the will to set up a defensive posture. Further, the perception of a threat can remain long after the real threat has been eliminated. Until the mere perception of the threat has also been eliminated, the person's will cannot change its direction. The will stays on defensive alert, and the etheric body remains in a concentrated state of defensive readiness. Once the individual believes that threats to her well-being are gone, she can wilfully shift her vibration out of its defensive posture. The intense concentration of etheric energies dissipate, and the etheric field opens.

From another perspective, the protective function calls upon the etherics to repel harmful light and energy with a vigour of resistance that conforms to the need of the moment. If the light frequencies entering the space of a manifest-form are impure and tainted with negativity, the etheric body responds by generating the appropriate configuration and polarity to repel them. Similarly, incoming frequencies can be pure and healthy, but incompatible with the etheric body's source-form. The etheric magnetic field is reconfigured to deal with incompatible frequencies. Whether impure or incompatible, the etheric field is encoded to act selectively upon unwanted frequencies with an appropriate measure of strength.

Incoming frequencies do not have to be unwanted or incompatible to be a problem. If light enters form in excessive amounts, it can also threaten form's integrity by causing form to melt or break down.

The etheric body is then called upon to generate strong and concentrated resistance. If strong enough, form's integrity remains intact. Answering to the need to resist means that the etheric body must repel an offending frequency with an intensity and quality of energy that matches the offending frequency's energy.

Incarnate individuals progress through their spiritual evolutionary process at their own speed. If an individual receives the quality and quantity of light she needs, balance is maintained. When incompatible frequencies or excessive amounts of light become a problem, the individual is likely to encounter undesirable life experiences. The spiritual path presents many situations where protection from excessive or undesirable light is necessary to maintain the integrity of the evolving spiritual devotee.

The speed of an individual's spiritual evolution needs to be appropriate for the individual. This means that the quantity and quality of light frequencies attracted and assimilated must match the individual's capacity to grow. If light is assimilated too slowly, the devotee will need to enhance her attraction for more and better frequencies. If too quickly, the devotee will be incapable of dealing with the overwhelming number of incoming higher frequencies. She will need the protection afforded by her etheric body. To keep an individual's spiritual progress on track, the etheric body must temper excesses and maintain balance in the face of an ever-changing external environment.

As an example of the way an etheric body protects the devotee on the spiritual path: fundamentalist Christians, orthodox Jews, or strict Muslims each provide their followers with a sheltered sanctuary in which to conduct their spiritual growth. The religion is clearly defined with doctrines and rules; it maintains strict boundaries. Within the confines of the sanctuary of the religion, the devotee is free of extraneous influences that could destabilize or even confuse her.

The devotee is protected by the external physical confines of the church's organizational structure, but is also protected by the attraction of compatible, as well as, the repulsion of incompatible light frequencies. The etheric body, emanating from the confines of the religion, enhances the space surrounding the religious sanctuary with its own etheric magnetic field. It prevents the intrusion of unwanted energies and opens the door to wanted energies. The devotee is therefore only exposed to light that conforms to the doctrines and boundaries set up by the religion. Growth can then take place in relative peace.

By working within the religious context, the combined strength of its members and leadership empowers the collective etheric magnetic field beyond the strength possible from the etheric field of a single individual. Even persons with weak etheric fields need not be concerned about the intrusion of disruptive negative energies. Their religion shelters and protects them.

In contrast, the spiritual teacher-devotee relationship can result in a much different outcome. The devotee may encounter difficulty working with frequencies outside of her comfort zone. The genuine spiritual teacher's light will be quite pure and positive, but the student's vibration may be too dense to receive it. When the light available is more than the student can handle, her etheric body will concentrate its magnetic field to create a block. If the block is adequate, the excessive incoming light will not threaten balance or otherwise upset stability and identity.

To protect herself, either consciously or unconsciously, the student acts to create separation from the teacher. She may get angry and leave in a fury; or she may leave without being noticed. If the student projects her discomfort onto the teacher, the teacher will need to be wise enough to remain detached. Her negative projection is merely another way to create separation and remove herself from the overwhelming flow of empowering light frequencies emanating from the teacher. Through separation, she provides herself with the space to assimilate and process those frequencies already acquired.

Automatically, the etheric body attracts and repels the exact range of frequencies that conforms to the devotee's current vibration. For the less evolved individual, fundamentalist religions augment the etheric body's limitation on incoming light. For others, separation from overwhelming light comes with an act of will or anger. If the spiritual seeker finds the correct amount and quality of light, growth is assured. If the light is beyond the etheric body's capacity, growth is precarious. For some devotees, both fundamentalist religions and the alignment to, or separation from, strong teachers secure the space needed to allow them to progress spiritually at their own speed.

*   *   *   *   *

An act of individual will has the power to both increase and decrease the intensity of the concentrated etheric field, but the role of the will encompasses more. The will comes from both conscious and unconscious sources. Among the advanced species on Earth, will springs from conscious free choice. You and I can choose to say "yes" or "no" to anything we encounter and then take action. For other species on Earth, however, conscious free choice is replaced by instinct. Whether choice is free or instinctual, it affects the individual's vibration, and consequently, the etheric magnetic field.

Survival of a species based on "instinct" is an exercise of will, but is directed by the higher-self. The rabbit survives the attack of the coyote, for example, because the will of the higher-self alters the rabbit's etheric field energies sufficiently to prevent the coyote from bringing enough of its intrusive negative intention to bear.

To repel the coyote's attack, the rabbit's higher-self projects the light frequencies needed for protection. The rabbit's etheric body both attracts and receives the light given, and it also interacts with its higher-self to communicate which frequencies are needed to create an effective defence. Thereafter, the rabbit's etheric field (on Earth) interacts with the coyote's etheric field to create disharmony. If the energies that empower the rabbit's etheric body are more powerful than the coyote's, the disharmony created will be adequate to prevent the coyote from entering the rabbit's space. The rabbit hops out of the way leaving the coyote frustrated.

When attempting to understand the outcomes created by the unconscious will, consideration must be given to the notion that both the coyote and the rabbit spring from the same source of Oneness. The same level of the common higher-self that sets up the etheric field of the rabbit also sets up the etheric field of the coyote. At one level, unconscious will appears to be separate, but at a higher level, unconscious will is controlled by the same source. Today the rabbit gets away, but tomorrow the coyote catches it. The will is programmed for survival, yet, because the will springs from the same source, the question is, who survives? The answer is found in the balance of nature. The common higher-self works through the etheric body to effect the balance of nature that it sees fit.

Conscious free-will, as compared to instinct, is limited to the perceptions of the physical plane and is programmed differently. Conscious will exists within the context of duality, and therefore within the context of separation. It is not shared in common. When one person assaults another person, the victim seeks to defend herself. Unless the higher-self is invited to participate, the drama of conflict involves only the energies of the physical plane. Higher-self cannot violate the conscious free-will on Earth by intruding without permission.

The outcome of conscious wilful conflict is dependant on whose etheric body is better able to repel the offensive energies of the other. The outcome is thereby determined by the will of the stronger.

To defend itself, the incarnate mind influences the etheric body, actively taking responsibility for the process. First, it draws upon the etheric energy that is immediately available. It shifts energy from one area of the etheric body to the area being defended. Second, the mind creates a number of new light frequencies. Because the creative power of the Godself is vested in the Oneness, the mind's own Oneness creates light. Light so created serves to empower and energize the etheric field to further repel offending frequencies. When the etherics are strong, stronger frequencies can be repelled. The mind uses both its ability to focus energy and its ability to create light from within to enhance the effectiveness of the etheric body.

The etherics are always involved with threats to well-being, but are not always able to cope. On a physical level, shouts of anger, car accidents, and violence present threats to well-being against which the magnetic field of the etheric body can do little to protect the individual. For protection, the individual would have to initiate physical response by moving away from the threat, or counter with offensive actions of her own.

The etheric body is the first layer of being-ness to be penetrated by threatening energies. It can detect the subtle energy of an approaching bus into its magnetic field before visual or auditory contact. By passing the energies received onto the mind, the etherics provide the mind with a warning. If the mind receives enough energy in time, the individual will consciously look for the bus and step out of the way. If not, a bus moves through a person's etheric magnetic field at highway speed unopposed—a messy prospect!

The etheric body uses the patterns of its magnetic configuration to attract and repel frequencies within a set range of vibration for protection. The integrity of the source-form, from which the etheric field emanates, is dependent on the etherics' ability to filter and control the flow of light moving into its space. When attraction and repulsion are not enough, the will can be brought to bear either consciously, through choices carried out by the mind, or unconsciously through the intervention of the higher-self. The will re-shapes the etherics to generate stronger resistance. If the etherics are strong enough, offending energies are repelled. If the offending energy is stronger, the defending entity will be drained of her energies or destroyed.

2.5 Change From Within

Manifest-form grows and evolves with every light frequency attracted by its etheric body. Because the etheric body emanates from its manifest-form, its vibrational rate and magnetic encoding are perfectly attuned to the form's needs. Only frequencies compatible with the form and its etheric field are able to harmonize sufficiently to be attracted. Because manifest-form determines which frequencies are attracted and repelled, the inspiration for change arises, not from any external source, but from within the form itself.

Have you ever found yourself attempting to help someone to satisfy your own perceptions of what that person needs? Have you ever found yourself thinking that another person's life could be better somehow if only that person did things a little differently?

The objective of helping another, whether or not the helping person is consciously aware, is to raise the other person's vibration. The means is the assimilation of light. Helping another person to assimilate light and raise his vibration is admirable, if the intent is free of vanity.

The belief that helping another person is our duty exemplifies change initiated from external sources. In a free-will zone such as the Earth, permission is mandatory. A person can only help another if that other person is first willing to be helped. The helper offers his own light frequencies in the form of suggestion. From the light offered, the receiving person takes the helper's suggestion and assimilates those frequencies to which his vibration is open. The receiving person, however, cannot assimilate incompatible frequencies. Frequencies that are too high and subtle or too low and dense are outside of the range of compatibility. How can the helping person possibly know which frequencies are compatible or not compatible? If the helping person cannot offer compatible frequencies, his efforts will be futile. One person can help raise the vibration of another, but only on condition that the receiving person's vibration be compatible with the light frequencies offered and that he is willing to be helped.

To use the colloquial, "you can lead a horse to water, but you can't make him drink". Perhaps the horse was hungry, not thristy.

On Earth, the exposure to light is not always harmonious. If a light frequency from an outside source is particularly strong, it can impose its influence—wanted or not. The imposing energy creates an imbalance within form, thus allowing the intrusion of a different set of light frequencies. As long as the imposition exerts greater energy than the etheric field, its influence will be effective. Forcing light frequencies upon someone, perhaps even forcing them to accept a new behaviour, effects change from the outside.

Whenever outside energies impose themselves upon the vibration of a manifest form or person, their influence is temporary. It lasts only until the affected vibration or person is strong enough to resist. The objective of the resistance is to correct the imbalance within form. To neutralize and remove unwanted energy, the source-form must empower and strengthen its etheric body by rearranging and concentrating etheric energy to enhance the field's ability to attract and repel light. The etheric body can then protect its source-form's integrity. Once the person or source-form has generated the vitality of vibration needed for repulsion, the outside influence becomes ineffective. The strength to resist comes from within.

For most manifest-forms on Earth, change from within takes place without any conscious involvement. The natural state of the source-form's vibration interacts with its environment to accept and slough off light energy that contributes to change. Change occurs without conscious effort with every frequency assimilated or released. Only the vibration of the source-form and its etheric body determine the frequencies attracted and repelled.

Change without conscious involvement tends to be basic. But in the human experience, conscious free-choice takes the process of change beyond the basics. When a person makes a conscious choice, the will, mind, and conscious body get involved. Our conscious choices direct and redirect the flow of light and energy. The ensuing manipulation of frequencies cause changes within the person's form. The form's changed vibration then emits a changed etheric field that attracts and repels the quantities and qualities of light and energy that conform to the person's changed vibration and therefore to the person's choice.

Since choices arise from within, from what possibilities may an individual choose?

The choices of a particular individual normally fall within a range that is consistent with the individual's current vibration. Each life situation has its own set of frequencies and vibrations different from every other life situation. People make choices that conform to the comfort of their own vibrations. Could the 17 year old fast-food cashier feel comfortable managing an electronics store? Could the manager of the electronics store feel comfortable dispensing financial planning advice? Could the financial planner feel comfortable arguing Plato's dialectic in philosophy class? Could the philosophy professor feel comfortable working at the fast food counter?

To choose outside of the scope of the familiar leads to uncertainty. A radical choice can create an anachronism within the evolutionary process by prompting the individual to jump from one environment of growth to a totally unrelated environment. The jump can upset or retard the process or push an individual along too quickly. Incarnate individuals make choices consistent with their vibrations because their choices place them among light frequencies that nourish their well-being and help them to evolve.

The reasons that motivate one choice over another are not always simple. The complexities of a person's current vibrational state must be understood at many levels before one can truly appreciate why he chooses as he does.

A client of mine came seeking to move forward on her spiritual path. She had a husband, two children, and aspirations to run for political office. From the first couple of personal sessions, it became clear that her growth was contingent upon her willingness to commit herself to her spirituality. The choice to commit determined how accelerated her spiritual path would be.

But the choice to commit and the resulting acceleration had consequences. Accelerated growth would have caused a major shift in her vibration. She would have moved beyond her husband's denser outlook, and marital separation was likely to follow. Spiritual commitment would have brought intense changes, as well as challenges for which she was not ready. Without any serious effort, she chose the familiar—the love she knew and was ready for. She chose her family and personal goals over the commitment to accelerated spiritual growth. Her spiritual growth will continue, but at a pace she can handle. At the moment of truth, when a choice is made, all of the factors affecting our will contribute to the direction we finally take.

As it was, my client was unwilling to commit herself to her spirituality. Her perception that my fee was too high allowed her to leave discontented. She needed to maintain her vibration at a level in harmony with her husband, family, and political ambitions. Her discontent had no other purpose than that of creating separation from me and the accelerated path. Her choice was made freely, and thereby, maintained her vibration in perfect balance with her life as it was. She came seeking accelerated spiritual growth and left with a greater realization of what was important to her. She made her conscious free-choice from within and chose what was best for her.

The impetus for change comes first from within, and is central to all vibration, even to vibration at its most basic level. Each individual makes choices according to what is right for self. If our vibration is unable to handle the brilliance of accelerated spiritual growth, spiritual growth comes at a slower pace. Growth follows the assimilation of one frequency at a time. The will to acquire higher and more subtle light frequencies must come from within and cannot be imposed.

2.6 The Interface Function

The etheric body projects for a significant distance into its immediate surroundings. The human etherics, for example, project up to 60 feet around the body and, beyond that, into the higher dimensions. When the etheric magnetic field projects into higher dimensions, it interfaces with the Oneness of the lighted universe to attract light in the same way as it does on Earth. Same role, different level. Because the etheric body is able to interface with both its immediate surroundings, as well as higher dimensional Oneness, the light available to its source-form is unlimited.

For an incarnate individual to bring light to Earth from the higher realms, she must first fulfill a few basic prerequisites. She must possess the ability to project her etheric field into the heavens. Projecting into the heavens beyond the Earth plane usually involves a meditation discipline. To make the choice to project her etherics, the individual must be sufficiently evolved to exercise free-will consciously. Very young souls on Earth have their hands full merely adapting to physical reality. Therefore, although young souls possess free-will, they are unlikely to use it to choose to transcend into higher levels of consciousness. Finally, the being's vibrational rate must be high enough to be compatible with the higher realms. Someone who attends prayer meetings, for example, has a much better chance of resonating with the heavens than someone who attends poker games. The basic prerequisites that put an individual into position to bring light from the heavens to Earth include meditation, choice, and vibration.

The etheric body attracts and repels light at every dimensional level in creation, and so, when an individual projects her etheric body into the heavens, she gains access to all of the frequencies of the lighted universe. Projecting involves the consciousness. The individual sitting quietly in meditation can centre her energies of consciousness, connect with her higher-self, and then move her consciousness into the heavens. When consciousness transcends, so too does its etheric magnetic field, which establishes itself in the heavens to attract light. If some of the light encountered is also compatible with the physical plane, it can be brought back to Earth for possible assimilation.

Although the etheric body can interface directly with the Oneness of the higher dimensions, most of its work is carried out on Earth interfacing with the etheric bodies of other individuals, groups, or energies. In any particular life situation, the quality of energy, the topics of conversation, the interests, the surrounding environment, and the focus are distinctly different from any other situation. The etheric interface provides the flexibility that allows most individuals to participate competently in many different life situations. Because each situation that an individual enters involves an entirely different set of frequencies, the etheric field is configured to work differently as well.

Consider the differences between a group of baseball players and a group of computer geeks. For computer geeks, typing skills, memory, and computer literacy are important. For baseball players, strength, agility, and balance are important. As different vibrations define each group, the configurations of their respective etheric fields reflect those differences. The quantity, quality, and range of light frequencies filtered by the etheric body of the computer geek are completely different than the frequencies filtered by the baseball player. But in the human experience, the baseball player can also be a computer geek, and the computer geek can also be a baseball player. The etheric body of any one person is capable of adapting to both groups, if she so chooses.

If an individual wanted to be both a computer geek and a baseball player, her etheric body would contribute by re-configuring or bending its magnetic field to create harmony in the baseball players' environment, and by re-configuring again to create harmony within the computer group environment. In each case, the etheric magnetic field adjusts to the light frequencies available in the space at hand, by accentuating certain aspects of its magnetic construct. It bends or re-balances its energies; it re-encodes its magnetic pulses to harmonize with the light available.

In every life situation encountered, the etheric body resets its magnetic codes to suit its immediate needs. It brings the vibration of its source-form, i.e., the person or object, into alignment with the object or environment from which the available light frequencies originate. The etheric body automatically shifts its magnetic field configuration from one situation to the next. The etheric body has versatility. It can help the same person to be both a baseball player and a computer geek. It can set us up to be anything we choose to be.

Driving a car provides another illustration of how the etherics work. The driver's conscious intent is to move from one destination to another. The vibrations of the traffic, the road conditions, the qualities of the vehicle, and all other aspects of the experience are reflected in the many etheric magnetic fields present in the driving environment. The driver's own etheric field interfaces and attempts to create harmony with each etheric field encountered.

Any shift in the energy, within the etheric fields of the driving environment, creates a shift in the energies acting upon the driver's own etheric field. Eventually, the shift becomes apparent to the driver's mind. When the traffic light turns green, energy will shift to tell the driver to move forward. The etheric magnetic field is the means by which the energy of the thought-forms related to the traffic light are transferred from the external environment into the driver's consciousness.

The alert driver's mind will easily recognize a shift of energies because her etheric field is highly attuned to what is happening around her. For example, her etheric field picks up the energies given off by the presence of another car in the adjacent lane and passes them on to the mind's consciousness and to its awareness. The alert driver then turns her head, without thinking, to see the other car beside her. The shifting energy found within the driving environment initially registers in the etheric magnetic field and is then relayed to the mind for processing. In contrast, the semi-alert driver will be less aware of what is going on around her. The semi-alert driver's etheric field is not attuned, is less sensitive to shifts in energy, and is unlikely to communicate with either the mind's consciousness or its awareness. Semi-alert drivers prompt the need for a horn that works, as compared to an etheric field that is sensitive.

The shift of magnetic energy allowing harmonization with the outer world takes place solely within the etheric body itself. But the etheric interface is magnetic, not conscious. Consciousness is not involved.

The key to the etheric magnetic interface is harmony. An object or manifest-form interfaces with all other objects and forms within its environment to the degree that harmony exists between them. Harmony allows the energies of one form to flow to and from another form. Without harmony, the etheric body blocks the establishment of an interface and creates separation. In effect, the etheric field closes to incompatible vibration and opens to compatible vibration harmoniously and automatically.

Harmony is defined differently in the heavens than on Earth. In the heavens, where all of creation is fully surrounded by love, one etheric body connects with another and their respective magnetic fields merge with ease. All heavenly form is Oneness, and although each etheric body retains its separate identity, it also fully joins in osmotic union with other etheric bodies. The light flows to and from joined forms without resistance or effort. On Earth, the etheric connection is governed by the same principles. Form, however, is not fully surrounded by love, nor is it fully present as Oneness. Some forms are evolved enough to possess the love and Oneness needed for their etheric bodies to merge harmoniously. For them, compatible light frequencies flow back and forth relatively easily. For others, the vibrations of their physical forms are dense and limited, and therefore, unable to establish an etheric interface with most other forms. Harmony in the heavens is assured by all-encompassing love, but on Earth, harmony occurs between compatible forms.

On Earth, harmony between one vibration and another evolves best within closed and protected environments. The closed environment is not bombarded by disturbing outside influences and is largely at peace.

For example, the marsh pond teems with plant and animal life. If left undisturbed, each member of the pond's ecosystem interacts with each other member in natural harmony. Light, energy, and vibration, however, do not ebb and flow freely without tension. Each individual etheric field precisely defines the quantity and quality of light and energy that it can attract and tolerate. The place, to which vibration flows within a closed ecosystem, is determined by one etheric body acting upon another, according to the balance of nature.

The human community is its own ecosystem and, like nature, is comprised of numerous subsystems. Each race, nationality, city, and neighbourhood thrives within its own natural harmony. As a given human community evolves, the parameters of harmony gain clarity. The etheric body is the mechanism for harmonious interface between the community members.

The capacity to generate the interface between any two living beings can be better understood after reviewing the etheric body's basic construct. The configuration of a being's etheric magnetic field nearest to its source-form is different than the configuration at its outer edges. Nearest to the source-form, the etheric body exists in perfect harmony and at the same rate of vibration as its source-form. At the outer edges, its magnetic field shifts to adapt to other etheric fields as they are encountered.

The amount of shift, and therefore, the range of other etheric fields to which adaptation is possible, is determined by the source-form's own vibration. If the source-form is evolved, it emanates an etheric body that can adapt easily. If unevolved, the etheric body will have difficulty reconfiguring its magnetic codes to harmonize with other etheric bodies. Because the etheric body interfaces with outside vibration at its outer edges, and remains in harmony with its source-form at its inner edges, the integrity of its source-form is unaffected by shifts on the surface of the etherics.

The purpose of the interface between two etheric bodies is to allow light frequencies to flow from one source-form to another freely. The quantity and quality of compatible light is regulated by the vibration of each of the merged source-forms. If the source-forms are evolved, higher and more subtle frequencies are exchanged. If the source-forms carry a great deal of density, only the slower and denser frequencies are exchanged. Regardless of the levels of evolution and density, when light moves back and forth through the etheric interface, the source-forms involved, whether persons or objects, are exposed to frequencies that enhance and empower their vibration. Just talk to a friend, and you will know how it works. Better yet, give her a hug.

The etheric body is able to adjust its configuration to work with light from the heavens and with light from any environment on Earth. By adapting to the immediate environment, or to the heavens, the etheric body interfaces with its external world. To the extent that physical density will allow, light flows through the interface as connected etheric magnetic fields make their exchange. The etheric body's source-form then has the opportunity to assimilate the frequencies to which it is exposed. As a particular being grows with the light it receives, its compatibility with other forms, beings, and environments expands. Each interface brings more light, and thereby, expands the range of life situations where interface becomes possible.

2.7 Etheric Blueprinting

The attraction and repulsion of light to and from the etheric body is determined by the vibration of its source-form and regulated by the codes inherent in its magnetic field. Every vibration is absolutely unique, as is the way it interacts with its environment. Etheric magnetic field encoding provides the unique blueprint by which every piece of creation harmonizes and fits together with every other piece. Etheric encoding is also used to record karmic responsibilities, as well as, astrological characteristics.

2.7.1 Karmic Encoding

Karma is applicable to beings of consciousness capable of exercising free-will, but only within our own third-dimensional space. Through action and reaction, individuals exchange negative and positive energies, and thereby, create and destroy karma. Karma is the means by which the universe keeps account of lessons yet to be learned. When a lesson is learned, karma is destroyed. When a lesson is outstanding, it affects our vibration, and in turn, affects the etheric body. Karma is directly encoded onto the etheric body with every shift in vibration due to action or reaction.

Karma holds us responsible for what we do. Karma comes from action. Action comes from the will. The will comes from the spontaneous pulses of energy that arise from within. Our actions are directed by the mind as it fulfils the desires of the will. Although the will is not always controlled by the consciousness, an individual is always responsible for what he does. Responsibility is derived from the principle that action is the creation of energy arising from the will. As our will is solely our own, we are solely responsible for its actions and subsequent karma.

The karmic encoding of the etheric magnetic field occurs whenever the vibration of its source-form experiences shifts in light frequencies and energy caused by action. When action is overwhelmingly harmonious or disharmonious, the shift causes an imbalance that affects the individual's life path. If disharmonious, the imbalance produces blockages in the etheric field. Blockages prevent both the attraction of some frequencies and the repulsion of others. As a result, the source-form is exposed to undesirable frequencies, while being denied access to desirable frequencies. Its vibration, and subsequent etheric field, become more dense. Consequently, the range of frequencies attracted and repelled are also more dense. Bad karma equals lower vibration, lower etheric vibration, and lower frequencies. When an individual generates disharmonious action, he creates bad karma, and in turn, sets up his life to head down the road instead of up.

Disharmonious action creates a unique magnetic code that is registered within the etheric magnetic field as "bad" karma. Encoded bad karma blocks an individual from being exposed to the higher light frequencies needed for spiritual growth. Clearing bad karma from the etherics requires the completion of life's lessons. Until cleared, any future lessons, as well as evolutionary progress, remain suspended. Clearing bad karma is not an option.

Karmic encoding upon the etheric body is created by action and is removed by action. Actions that remove the magnetic codes of bad karma re-balance the etheric body. Removing a karmic code caused by dishonesty means learning honesty. To correct the imbalance caused by dishonest action, a person must act honestly. His honest act must be strong enough to neutralize the offense. Through redeeming action, the dishonest person demonstrates that he has learned honesty. Once the lesson is complete, the formerly dishonest person's vibration rises high enough to clear the karmic code from the etheric body.

Does anyone get away with anything? Ever?

Etheric codes are automatically imprinted on the etheric body at the moment offensive action takes place. The thief that steals a car carries the full complement of codes that go with the lessons of stealing, starting at the moment he commits the crime. The accounting process can be compared to accounting procedures at the local bank, except that the etheric body's balance sheet is far more precise and can never be misplaced.

As the thief inevitably comes to the moment when he must repay his debt, in this lifetime or another, there is no need for the victim of the crime to be vindictive or seek revenge. If the victim does so, his own negative actions of revenge are also automatically registered on the etheric body. Seeking revenge attracts bad karmic encoding because the lesson begs to be learned. Although the thief never gets away with stealing, neither does the victim ever get away with revenge. Because of etheric encoding, escaping our transgressions is impossible. No one gets away with anything ever.

A karma-producing action means that the etheric magnetic field carries a distortion that perverts the flow of energy and light. Completion of the lesson corrects the distortion, dissipates the etheric imbalance, and alters the magnetic code thus removing the karmic debt. By correcting the distortion, the flow of light and energy resume their normal patterns.

In contrast, when a person acts positively to create "good" karma, the result is greater harmony. Good karma causes the etheric field to vibrate faster. Greater harmony and faster vibration translate into the attraction and assimilation of higher and more subtle light frequencies. More light equals more spiritual growth. There is no telling how far a random act of kindness can move a person forward towards enlightenment, or how much it contributes to harmony on Earth.

Karmic encoding plays an integral role in the interaction between individuals. The etheric field is intimately involved in the way beings are able to connect with each other. The etheric body of one person merges with the etheric body of another. If there is harmony, interaction is positive. Without harmony, the etherics do not merge, but repel, causing each person to go his own way in life.

When one person acts in an offensive manner towards another, he creates a karmic distortion in the etheric fields of both persons. Whenever the same two parties come into close proximity, the encoded distortion causes the etheric magnetic fields of both individuals to grate against each other. Cordial socializing with someone who owes you a karmic debt is made very difficult by the disharmony inherent to both etheric fields.

Correction of the encoded disharmony occurs when the offender repays his "debt". If the offender stole money from the victim, repayment means giving it back. If the offender verbally abused the victim, an apology might do. Corrective action is necessary to re-balance the etherics. The victim's vibration eliminates the etheric blockage to the presence of the offender's vibration; and the offender resumes his place on his life-path to continue his spiritual growth.

Direct repayment of karma means that the offender makes reparations through positive actions involving the victim. The victim, however, may not want to have anything further to do with the offender. He has the option to release his connection with the offender by simply asking the universe to take over the debt. Asking through meditation or prayer is the usual method.

When the universe takes over the offender's debt, the negative energy experienced by the victim is replaced by positive energy and the victim moves on. Thereafter, the offender's debt repayment plan does not involve the victim; and any positive actions related to the outstanding lesson can be applied to re-balance the etheric body. When the universe takes over from the victim, however, the debt is likely to be discharged sooner, and the demands upon the offender will be more rigorous. Whether repaid directly to the victim or indirectly to the universe, karmic debt cannot be avoided.

Offensive actions that create bad karma are defined by the universe and not by the perceptions of either the offender, the victim, or anyone else. What constitutes an offending, and thereby, karma-producing action? In general terms, karma results from the violation of the universal standards of good conduct. The implication involves the "view-from-heaven" which, of course, comes void of ego and

Earthly illusions. What is good conduct? Perhaps the most time-honoured approach to the answer is to take to heart the golden rule: do unto others as you would have them do unto you. Common sense is a good measure of good conduct.

The acid-test for karma-producing action is based on love. Does an individual's vibration violate love or does it enhance love? While the Earthly mind's perception of right and wrong is often clouded by ego and illusion, God knows without question. Appropriate and inappropriate actions are precisely and objectively recorded on the etheric magnetic field without fail or prejudice.

The universe has many objectives. Assessing the rightness or wrongness of our every action is very difficult. What does God really have in mind for us? How shall we interpret unfolding events?

A person may act in what seems to be a very harsh and cruel way towards another person. If his action is wilful and conscious, he is responsible. But if his action arises from uncontrollable spontaneity, the higher-self is responsible. In effect, the higher-self directs the person's actions, which are, therefore, divinely inspired no matter what they appear to be on the surface. Action arising from the higher-self produces no karma. On the other hand, if the action is wilful, it arises from self and karma is certain. Without clarity about how and why we act as we do, imposing judgements upon ourselves is less than wise.

Karma teaches. By creating an impersonal system of credits and debts, karma makes learning our lessons unavoidable. The forms that lessons take reflect the way that the dramas of learning need to unfold. Even when we act inappropriately and are responsible, making judgements on one's self is counter-productive. Karma-producing actions serve as both a prompt for recognizing the lesson-at-hand and a prompt to work it through. The system of karmic credits and debts is purposeful. The purpose is to facilitate learning—not to chastise.

The automatic registration of actions and reactions on the etheric body leaves an unavoidable record of karmic credits and debts. The absolute precision with which every nuance of action is recorded leaves nothing unseen. As every action is known completely and is immediately recorded in the etherics, we are not merely responsible for our actions, we are also held accountable. The etherics are quite "foolproof". To think there is an escape from the repayment of crimes is folly.

Karma is impermanent. The destruction of karmic debts comes with the learning of lessons. Each completed lesson opens both the etherics and the individual to the light frequencies introduced by the lesson. Karma can also be destroyed in the presence of love. Love is like the holy temple reserved for enlightened beings. Those who come into its space are showered with the light of divine grace. Light removes the encoded karmic distortions found in the etheric field and corrects the imbalances that impede spiritual progress.

Learning the lessons, that eliminate karma, attracts light, yet the greatest lesson is love. With love, comes an abundance of light. In the presence of love and light, particular lessons lose their importance. When our beings transcend the density of this plane through love, karma soon disappears.

2.7.2 The Miracle of Birth

The human physical body is occupied by the spirit of the soul—one only.

The potential for a particular body to be plagued by the presence of more than one spirit exists if the etheric body is weak. For instance, being possessed by demons, having multiple personalities, or experiencing delusions of grandeur can be better understood as the invasion of negative spirits into a weak etheric body with holes in its magnetic field. In contrast, being a "walk-in" can be better understood as the withdrawal of the original soul-spirit from the physical body, after which, a second soul enters the body to complete the life. A "walking-in" takes place through agreement between souls and does not subject the body to negative or unwanted energies against the host's will. A third situation involving one body and two spirits occurs during the miracle of birth. Until the fetus exits the womb and separates from the mother, the newborn's soul is not allowed to enter its body.

Reproduction does not occur in a state of disharmony. The principle that protects a woman from experiencing the inappropriate and premature invasion of her future baby's spirit is the agreement between souls to respect the sanctity of the mother's body. By agreement, the spirit-light of the incoming newborn remains disengaged from the physical body until birth when the fetal body separates from the mother's body.

If the baby's spirit enters before physical separation, the presence of two different spirits within the same body creates confusion within the mother. With both spirits expressing through the mother's body in different and conflicting ways, the integrity of the mother is severely compromised. Harmony within the mother's body is maintained, however, by the soul-level agreement that ensures that the newborn's spirit enters its body only after effective physical separation.

The divine process of reproduction cannot allow the confusion of multiple spirits in the same body. Who is at the helm while the mother is pregnant? The mother's soul, not the baby's, has propriety over her body. Birth is a most holy and sanctified event that allows spirit from the divine enlightened universe to manifest on Earth.

The respect given to the mother's body and her spirit are nothing less than the will of God. Although the incoming spirit is welcome to be nearby during conception and pregnancy, entry to the body occurs only at birth.

The need for physical separation does not imply the same need for etheric separation. At the moment the baby's spirit enters its fetal body at birth, the newborn emanates its own very unique etheric body. If the baby's etheric field remains within the mother's etheric field even for a brief moment, the integration of their etheric bodies is so thoroughly intimate that the process of bonding is much stronger. Bonding is further strengthened if the baby is given to the mother to hold directly from the womb *before* the baby leaves the mother's etheric field. Without separation, their etheric magnetic fields merge to become thoroughly encoded with each others' spirit-light.

In the immediate moments after birth, although it is necessary that the physical bodies be separate, separation of the etheric bodies is neither necessary, nor desirable. The miracle of birth is more miraculous when we, as human spirits, understand how it works. Giving a baby to its mother directly from the womb is so simple, and its lifelong consequences are so profound.

2.7.3 Astrological Encoding

The etheric body carries the encoding of an incarnate individual's astrological blueprint. How so?

The answer starts with an understanding about where the incarnate spirit comes from and how it got to Earth. To begin, the Godhead extends itself into all of creation as manifestations of form at every level of being-ness. As soon as any level of creation is empowered by the assimilation of divine light, it becomes Oneness inherently possessing the God-given power to create. When Oneness uses its powers to create, creation expands into a multitude of new forms. In effect, the Godhead creates the creation; the creation creates more creation, including the soul; and the soul creates incarnate individuals.

To bring the incarnate body to life, the Oneness of the soul extends into the fetal body at the moment of birth. The soul enters the body at a very precise time and place on Earth after making the journey through the universe from where it dwells. Along the way, the soul's Oneness passes through numerous star systems and solar systems, passes by untold numbers of planets, and traverses galaxy after galaxy and dimension after dimension. The incarnating spirit follows a linear path from its origin in the heavens to its destination on Earth.

Every heavenly body in the universe, including stars, galaxies, solar systems, and planets, emanates an etheric magnetic field that imposes its influence upon the soul's Oneness as it journeys to Earth. Even the etheric body of the Earth imposes its influence. The soul's Oneness passes into and out of one etheric field after another. By the time the soul's Oneness arrives on Earth, it has been pruned, shaped, and imprinted with the characteristic vibration of each galactic etheric field encountered along the way. The little boy or girl that emerges from the womb carries the soul's spirit-light, which precisely mirrors the influences of the heavens at the time of birth.

To clarify, astrological influences affect the vibration of the incoming soul's spirit-light. They are felt through the etheric body because both the etherics and the influences are magnetic in nature. A particular influence will temporarily alter or reconfigure the etheric magnetic field, which then works to attract and repel light frequencies that conform to its new configuration. The frequencies attracted act upon the vibration of the soul's spirit-light to create real changes. Because the etheric field emanating from the vibration of the spirit-light perfectly reflects the spirit-light's vibration, it carries the imprint of all the astrological influences present.

Astrological influences continuously exert influence upon the etheric magnetic field of a person throughout his life. Initially, the influence is upon the etherics of the soul's spirit-light as it journeys through the heavens. Once the spirit-light has merged with the body of the newborn, the influence affects the etherics of the newborn on Earth. Astrological influences on the etherics are always changing, and are therefore temporary, but the effect on the person's vibration of the light frequencies attracted by the 'astrologically-influenced' etherics is real.

Astrologists have been able to calculate the influences specific to particular planets within our own solar system. A Mercurial presence in an astrological chart usually means a quickness of mind; the presence of Mars can indicate how a person's energies present themselves. Astrological calculations are also able to describe the combined influence of a number of planets. Unfortunately, calculating the influences of heavenly bodies and systems located beyond our own solar system has not been as easy. Although these influences are far more numerous, the science of astrology has third-dimensional physical limitations. It has yet to explain all of the influences within our own solar system. Understanding the influences of heavenly bodies outside our system is, for now, beyond our reach.

The moment that an incarnating spirit enters the physical body, defines the influences imprinted upon the newborn's etheric body. The place and time of birth is unique. The exact configuration of cosmic influences, as determined by the positions of the planets and star systems at the instant the spirit enters the body, is unique and cannot reoccur ever again. Each influence is imprinted automatically as the spirit journeys from its source in the soul to the incarnate body. The spirit-light of the incoming soul is also unique throughout all of creation. Birth brings all of the influences imprinted upon spirit into a singular expression of human being-ness.

The influences of the astrological blueprint upon the etheric body are greatest at the moment of birth. They are fresh and unchallenged; and the etheric codes are most clearly defined. This blueprint from birth exerts substantial influence throughout the individual's lifetime, but all things change. Birth is only one moment in time. The influences existing at birth begin to change in the first instance after birth and continue changing throughout the process of life.

Many catalysts initiate change. Among the first are our parents. Parents (or guardians) interact with us exposing us to their etheric magnetic fields, and then take us places where other etheric fields impose their influences. As an individual matures past adolescence, he assumes responsibility for his own life-path. Through the exercise of his free-will, he encounters other influences that can also change the etheric field configuration.

Changes happen every time a person is exposed to different light frequencies. Life's lessons bring new frequencies. Learning responsibility or self-esteem, for example, can profoundly alter the codes of the etheric body. Any time a new frequency is assimilated into the physical body, our vibration, etheric body, and etheric codes all change from what they were in the moment before. The original astrological etheric blueprint encoded at birth retains much of its influence throughout life, but its influence soon merges with the many other influences encountered on Earth.

Looking at the process of incarnation from an Earthly viewpoint is different than looking from the viewpoint of the heavens. From Earth, the model of birth, as described in the preceding passages, involves the linear journey of the incarnate spirit from its original source of the soul in the higher heavens to the emerging fetal body on Earth. The influences imposed upon the incarnating spirit occur as the spirit moves through time and space. Spirit traverses the distance between the soul in the heavens and the body on Earth; its journey begins at the time of departure and ends at the time of birth. From an Earthly perspective, the astrological influences affecting the incarnating spirit-light are fixed in Earth-time. They are calculated by referencing the positions of the heavenly bodies at the time of birth.

From the perspective of the heavens, however, the departure of the soul's spirit-light and its arrival in the physical body happen in unified time and, therefore, simultaneously. Until spirit-light crosses the dimensional threshold to enter the physical plane, it exists in a state of unlimited space and unified time. It exists everywhere at once and forever. Every cosmic influence that generates an imprint on the newborn's etheric body exists now and forever and here and everywhere. Earthly time and space are irrelevant. The incarnating spirit-light does not need to journey through time and space to be affected.

But as spirit-light enters the physical plane, it comes into the now-moment on Earth separate from the past and the future. It enters physical space at a fixed location relative to the location of the planets and heavenly bodies that have influence. Thereafter, cosmic influences are seen as being physically separate from each other, as well as from all other influences that have had an effect or are yet to be encountered. Because of the density of the physical plane, cosmic influences that exist in divine union in the heavens appear to us through the illusion of separation.

Every etheric field encountered along the journey to Earth provides its own influence upon the incarnating spirit-light, and therefore, upon its etheric body. The unchallenged uniqueness of the configuration of planets and star systems at the time of birth is perfectly preserved in the etheric body's encoded magnetic field. As beings on Earth act upon their environment, the etheric field guides the flow of light according to its encoded patterns, thereby giving weight to astrological influences. If going beyond our local solar system, and the limited perceptions of the third dimension, were possible, the influences of the galaxies, planets, and stars in the higher heavens might also be included in the calculations of astrology.

The etheric body is integral to the expression of manifest-form. The etherics stabilize and protect form and provide a means by which it can interact with other forms. Its intimacy with its source-form, as well as its many imprinted codes, determine the quantity and quality of light flowing within its magnetic field. Because all light frequencies available for assimilation into form must first pass through the etheric magnetic field, understanding the etheric body is crucial to the story of light.

Chapter 3: Starting From Scratch

3.1 How Do You Choose?

Each incarnate human being is born to the Earth as an emanation of his soul; and each soul came into being as an emanation of the higher unified soul for all of humanity. As each of us stepped down from the heavens into the lower dimensions and finally onto the Earth, we brought with us our own individual purpose. Our personal mission and our life path was prescribed by the collective human soul, as well as by our own soul, and was encoded deeply within. Each of us has come to fulfill the will of God to empower and enlighten the Earth in our own special way.

Coming to live on Earth was our choice, and fulfilling the will of God is also our choice. Earth was created as a place of free-will. Each of us can choose the darkness or the light. We were given the choice to complete our mission by joining our physical bodies with the light of the enlightened self or to remain separate. Heavenly beings are not allowed to intervene on our behalf, except where we permit them to do so. Our collective mission began in the heavens when we chose to serve the will of God, and our personal mission on Earth begins when we, as individuals, again choose to serve the will of God.

Unlike other species, we were given the freedom to conduct our mission by adapting our physical world to suit ourselves. Ours is the power of the physical plane. Our light is imbibed within all that we do. We are the manipulators of physical reality. We are the creators of our own world. As our spirit-light touches all that we are and all that we do, the image of God expresses through us and into our creations.

We are perfect extensions of the divine presence. As we continue to create a place of physical vibration for the coming of more and more light, our mission moves forward. We have the power and free-will to create our own destruction, and we have the power and free-will to create heaven on Earth.

Excitement can be found within the creation of our own reality. I have always been impressed that I can press the "enter" key on my computer summoning all the words that have passed through me into *The Story of Light*. We are creating physical reality on Earth; the words and the computer are the manifestations of our success. They are physical and fully separate within the duality in which we exist. Words and the computer are expressions of the image of God created on this physical plane. We can fully choose or not choose to celebrate our achievements and our creations. We are truly free. We are free to exclude ourselves from the lighted universe. And yet, we are free to choose the light as well.

Hallelujah! I am that I am. I choose, therefore, I am. I choose not, therefore, I am not. How do you choose? Each of our souls in the heavens has chosen to serve the light, and, if we on Earth choose again to serve the light, our mission begins.

3.2 The Physical Body

The most immediate task after choosing to serve on Earth was that of gaining a presence as physical beings in a physical world. Humanity needed a vehicle, a body into which spirit could come and learn about the third dimension. And so began the first adventure. How was it that our spirit-light came onto the planet? How was it that we should commune with the heavens from the physical plane? How was it that we were to bring heaven to Earth and complete our mission? The answers were to be found on Earth, in physical presence, in the incarnate body.

During the initial attempts to anchor light on Earth, the angels and Earth's light-workers subscribed to numerous misconceptions about the physical plane's ability to assimilate light. Much had to be learned. Assimilation needed light, but because the Earth's etheric body filtered out all but the very slowest and most dense frequencies, light was hard to come by. What to do? What worked, what did not work? The problems encountered eventually yielded to the solutions.

Light-workers experimented and innovated. To begin, the body that was to carry spirit-light had to survive within a physical context. Light-workers constructed the first physical bodies, then observed their creations. What type of body was capable of withstanding the rigours of a third-dimensional existence?

The assimilation of light into the physical body depended upon a biological construct. If the body was faulty or defective, the potential to assimilate light went unrealized. The body had to be designed to be compatible with third-dimensional vibration. Many prototypes were sent to stock the Earth. The knowledge acquired allowed the angelic caretakers of the Earth to improve upon their previous creations.

The first attempts to create the physical body had to keep Earth's early reality in perspective. Because the light available on Earth is determined by the state of the planet's etheric body, original designs recognized the need to accept frequencies within the limited range available. Therefore, initial constructs were most primitive.

Cave man, neanderthal man, and other early forms of the human body were not designed with the ability to accept light in the sophisticated ways inherent to the current human form. In those early times, the primary design focus was to produce a body that stood up to the problems of third dimensional physical endurance. Indeed, the cave man readily tolerated heat, cold, wet, and foul conditions. As well, the atmosphere that pervaded the Earth offered a much lower oxygen content. With less oxygen, the ability to convert vibrational frequencies into useable physical energy was not nearly as evolved as it is today. The body had to be designed for the conditions found on Earth.

As problems came up to be resolved, the angelic caretakers of the Earth learned how the body needed to function in the physical context. They developed the system of "fight-or-flight" for responding to fear. When the individual perceived a threat to her well-being, the adrenal glands infused a sudden boost of adrenalin into the body. Heart and respiration rates jumped, and the energy from the adrenalin better enabled the individual to escape danger. As another example, the nervous system was designed with voluntary and involuntary response controls (sympathetic and parasympathetic). The conscious mind controlled some of the body's function's, while other functions became automatic. In addition, blood vessels were placed in protected areas, sweat glands became part of the body's temperature-control system, and ear wax repelled insects. Many complex innovations were needed to make the body functional.

The task of making improvements to the human body was comparable to the designing of the automobile. Each innovation had to be tested, and, if it needed further improvement, the prototype went back to the factory. First, the human body was assembled as potential vibration in the heavens, then it manifested on Earth where its design features were tested. Each successful innovation was incorporated into the body, and each unsuccessful innovation was re-evaluated then redesigned or discarded. When the body needed improvements, it was "re-called" to the heavens, reconditioned, and the new-improved version was then sent back to Earth for further testing. Like the automobile, each improvement to the human body made the journey on Earth that much more pleasant.

Although a new and different model car is introduced to the public each calendar year, its basic design always includes four wheels, a steering wheel, and a driver's seat. Each new model represents all previous design improvements as the end product of an evolutionary process. The human body is also redesigned from time-to-time thus introducing a new and different model onto the Earth. But similar to the automobile, the human body has basic design features common to all models: a thumb in opposition, placement of the ears, eyes, nose, and mouth, and an upright torso with two legs. Each new model represents the improvements made to all previous models.

Early designs of the human body and its subsequent improvements have provided a great deal of interest to anthropologists. Changes to skull shape, height, spine curvature, foot size, and arm length among others, each demonstrate the march of evolution. In the beginning, the body was designed to handle difficult conditions. As time progressed, the Earth changed, and so too, did the function of the body. Each step forward allowed the body to work with more and more light. Although the basic design of the body remains the same, like the automobile, each innovation contributes to evolutionary change. When the body is recalled to the heavens for reconditioning, a completely different version is introduced to Earth. Both the Ford Model A car and the latest Lincoln Continental have four wheels, but can we say they are the same? How does the latest human body design differ from the body that survived the Ice Age?

The process of improving a species' vibration on Earth can be illustrated using the example of the Dodo bird. The Dodo bird manifested onto the Earth with unacceptable flaws only to become extinct early in the nineteenth century. It was unable to adapt to the physical plane using the body it had, and so, its essence was returned to its higher dimensional origins and reunited with its higher-self. The vibration of the physical Dodo was then reconditioned, after which, the improved version was sent back to the Earth.

The new form of the Dodo became the hybrid of an established Earth species[1]. Hybrid breeding was able to produce a distinctly unique DNA code that suited the new physical form of the improved Dodo bird. From an Earthly viewpoint, the new-improved Dodo is unrecognizable. From the heavens, the new version is seen as an alteration in the original creation. Improvements to both the vibration of the spirit-light and the manifest-form of the original Dodo bird are the result of the divine will to bring to Earth functional

1 Fortunate or unfortunate, my channelled source of information, the Councilate of the Ascended-Light, has chosen not to disclose which hybrid species the Dodo became. The point of the discussion focuses on the recall, reconditioning, and re-manifestation of species unsuitable for life on Earth. Any attempt to alter the conditions of our environment to prevent the recall (i.e., extinction) of an unsuitable species frustrates the process of divine improvement. Let them become extinct. If they are to serve the Earth, their spirit will return with a better body.

forms of being that can make a contribution to enlightenment.

Humanity has also undergone changes. During Earth's earliest time, the human physical body was designed to withstand and survive. The climate on Earth, the dense vibration, the lack of light, all made survival the first priority, and therefore, survival was the first design concern.

Reproduction was paramount to survival. Given the very harsh conditions on Earth, species reproduction was precarious at best. Initially, the body was designed with an extremely high-energy sex-drive. Strong drive ensured that man and woman copulated with adequate frequency. If the infant mortality rate was 9:10, ten pregnancies yielded one viable human. Although sex drive was essentially a matter of numbers, it was necessary to maintain survival.

The innovation that revolutionized the physical body was the incorporation of love into the primary driving force for reproduction. Love accelerates the vibrational rate of form, thus opening it to accept and assimilate more light.

The early versions of the body, prior to the infusion of love into the reproductive function, were fixed and limited in the amount of light with which they were capable of working. Having been designed for survival, the body had no chakras to empower. It had no connection to its higher-self, and no connection to a sustaining and nourishing source of divine light. The limitations of the unlighted body soon became apparent. It was unable to adapt to changes in its environment. It was not capable of transforming and evolving. At some point, the limited prototype had to be replaced by an improved prototype. Versions of the earliest primates appeared, then disappeared. Australopithecus man appeared, then an improved prototype replaced the first—Australopithecus Africanus, and a further improvement replaced the second—Australopithecus Aferensis, or so the story goes. Primitive man was eventually replaced by the early versions of modern man.

The difference love made to the evolutionary process of the body was the infusion of built-in adaptability. With love, light could be assimilated more readily. More light meant more Oneness. Oneness, as outlined in chapter one, has the inherent power of the God-self and the contingent power to create. Empowered by love, the body's Oneness created its own modifications on Earth without having to be recalled or replaced by an improved prototype. When love was included as a constituent of reproduction, humanity acquired the power to recreate itself to suit its environment.

3.3 Inventing the First Chakra

Bringing light to Earth proved to be a formidable challenge. The severity of the problems encountered on Earth could not have been anticipated. Earth's place was at the lowest and slowest level of vibration yet known to the lighted universe and farther into the void than any other vibration had ever journeyed. Although progress was exceptionally slow, light and form combined to create Oneness in scattered places on the planet.

Once the physical body had been adapted to the environment, experiments began for the purpose of anchoring light. In the heavens, bodies are made entirely of light. But, in the early days of Earth, invoking even an unnoticeable amount of light into the physical body occurred more through chance than intent. How could the physical body be adapted to assimilate light?

The few angelic light beings, who first scouted Earth's third dimension, came in their full presence as bodies of light. It was initially thought that the light-body could imbibe itself into the human physical body without difficulty. The physical body, however, was poorly designed for its role in a third-dimensional environment, and was simply not designed for the purpose of accommodating light frequencies, including the slow, low, and dense light frequencies found on Earth. Experiments began; numerous body types were created; their design features were tested for light-holding capabilities; and then, the body was abandoned for other improved versions. Fossils and more fossils. With each creation, the process of bringing the light-body into the physical body inched forward.

Although the challenge was overwhelming, the Earth's angelic light-workers had God's favour, and so, the work of enlightenment proceeded. God's will would inevitably prevail.

The first question was: where did the body hold light already? Experiments followed. In one experiment, crystals were implanted in the vain hope that the body would assimilate light. In another, light was manipulated and altered in the hope of making it compatible with the body. And in yet another, the Earth's light-workers created a concentrated beam, with which to bath the individual in light. Although none of these early experiments stood out as a success. Some light was capable of establishing within some structures in some areas of the physical essence. So, the angelic hosts investigated further.

Findings showed that light frequencies could be placed in the body only in particular locations and only at the molecular level. Further findings showed that bodily essence, not assigned to specific functions, retained light better than essence that had other specific functions. As the angelic hosts examined more deeply, they also found that if bodily essence was used for physical work or movement or fulfilled other physical demands, its ability to hold light was negligible. Bodily essence could not be used for both physical needs and spiritual needs simultaneously.

The investigation then deepened. Where could the body hold light?

Areas of the body that already held light were looked at more closely to see what might be learned. The discovery was soon made that the parts of the body that held light best were located at juncture points. Although the part-in-question was not functional, it was usually centrally located in relation to other functional parts. The discovery was also made that no single aspect of bodily essence was more or less capable of holding light than any other aspect. Points of juncture held more light because more light passed through them.

Points of juncture had another important feature. Because they were non-functional, their essence was inherently calm and undisturbed. Subtle and delicate frequencies of light needed a settled and peaceful space within which to merge with physical vibration. In a state of peace, harmony between light and form became possible.

Juncture points were sanctuaries of peace and therefore able to hold the light that passed through them.

Experiments in body design revealed that prominent juncture points were exposed to more light and that the essence therein shone with greater illumination. Juncture points were then re-designed to incorporate the principles that had been learned. Subsequent experiments proved that infusing light into the physical body's essence amounted to moving light back and forth over the same area, and especially over peaceful juncture points.

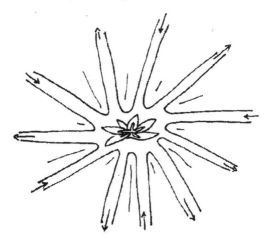

Juncture Points

Juncture points soon gained even more attention. They became the centres of light for ever higher and more subtle light frequencies. As further experiments yielded greater insight and as juncture points became more sophisticated, the new light centres came to be known as "chakras".

The guardian angels of Earth endeavoured to create the chakras within the body. Different chakra prototypes were placed into areas of the body that had demonstrated the highest levels of light flow. Eureka! With the new prototypes, light entered the body. Initial placements involved a three-chakra system including the base, heart, and crown chakras, which were not even linked to each other. The successes continued. What had begun as the observation of juncture points, led to the creation of chakras, and a major step forward in the quest to enlighten the human body.

Next came the discovery of physical essence that was capable of accepting light. Some physical tissues existed in either the third or the fourth dimensions and were also able to cross back and forth between dimensions. Although these tissues often vacillated between dimensions, they existed primarily in the third. Their ability to remain in physical form, however, was challenged whenever higher light frequencies were forced into the body. In response, the body's vibration immediately rose and popped out of the third dimension into the fourth dimension.

Because the problem of vibrational stability was acute, further experimentation was required. Courageous light-workers volunteered to incarnate onto the Earth to find the answers. By placing carefully measured amounts of light into the body, the threshold point, at which light crossed-over from the physical plane into the next higher dimension, could be determined. The physical body was then observed during the process to see which parts of the body's essence remained in the third dimension the longest prior to moving up into the fourth dimension. The bodily forms that were most capable of holding the light, while still remaining in the third dimension, became the physical substance used to create the chakras.

The chakras' essence-form was at once divine, but more important, they held light and stayed on Earth. The frequency rate of the chakras was specific and could be duplicated, thus allowing the angelic hosts to create the physical essence of the chakra light-centres here on Earth.

Initial successes in combining light with physical form depended upon using the highest and fastest vibrations of physical form and the lowest and slowest frequencies of light. Only the slowest light frequencies stood any chance of being assimilated. Because faster vibrations of form were able to manifest onto the Earth, and because light frequencies could be slowed down sufficiently, the initial invocations of light took place.

3.4 The Seed-Light

With the invention of the chakras, the body was able to accept light into its physical essence, and some light was assimilated. As the body received light, its Oneness grew. However, accepting a few light frequencies into the body is not nearly the same as accommodating the spirit-light of the soul. Although the body acquired light, further developments had to take place before the soul could also be used to enlighten the physical body.

For some time after their arrival on Earth, the vanguard of Earth's inhabitants remained in their bodies of light in the dimensions above the physical plane. The gulf between Earth's third dimension and the lowest dimensions to which the volunteer angelic light-workers were able to descend was enormous. The angels had come from the beyond, and even the beyond the beyond, into the lower heavens to be met with density that was incomprehensible. Descending to Earth was impossible; much had to be learned.

At the beginning of the densification process, Earth's volunteer light-workers retained their places in the heavens, but descended a little at a time. Being unable to fully descend onto the physical plane provided them with the advantage of enlightened vision. The view from above afforded the opportunity to survey Earth's vibration and to understand what had to be done. Remaining in the higher dimensions provided enlightened insight, but, once the process of densification got underway, the advantage diminished.

As they moved into physical form, the volunteer angelic light-workers attempted to retain their connection with their bodies of light by using the tools of light such as crystals, energy robes, wands, energy-enhancing structures, and geographical light-stations. By surrounding herself in light using one of the light tools[2] or a combina-

---

2 In this age of enlightenment, numerous incarnate light-workers are remembering how to build crystal wands, how to use crystals, and are receiving records of wisdom that were stored away in ancient times. The use of the copper energy bed or copper pyramid is a practice that has now been rediscovered as a means to compensate for physical

tion thereof, the volunteer light-worker could extend her vibration farther onto the physical plane. The tools compensated for some of the differences in vibration, thus allowing the volunteer to be partially physical, and yet, still connected with her light-body.

For a time, Earth's volunteer's made excursions into density, collected information, and then returned without fully entering the physical plane. The knowledge base of the third dimension grew significantly, but the limitations soon became apparent. At a certain point in the descent into matter, physical density became too great, and the tools of light became ineffective.

When the time came to move fully onto the physical plane, the tools of light had to be stored away. Humanity then fell into the great pit of Earth's physical density, and had to separate from its truth in the higher dimensions. As the journey into density thickened, memory of the higher-self and the lighted universe faded and became veiled in the illusions of the physical plane. The advantages of enlightened vision and the connections with the light-body were lost.

Immersion into physical form was the greatest sacrifice possible for a light-worker to make. Bodies of light could not tolerate the extreme density of the third dimension. These beings abandoned their physical bodies, whereupon they returned to the lighted realms. The light-workers who remained had come to Earth only to be profoundly separated from their higher-selves, from the enlightened universe, and from the knowledge of who they were in the heavens. In effect, they were marooned on Earth.

How could spirit be expressed on the physical plane? What would it take to effectively assimilate the soul's light into the human body? Without knowing how to bring the soul into the body, the light-workers embarked upon a new phase of innovation and experimentation.

One of the first innovations to be attempted involved the in-

---

density and to accelerate the physical vibration. As individuals awaken to enlightened living in the current epoch, the tools of light are once again helping to raise our vibrations.

vocation of spirit-light[3] into the human body during young adult-hood after the individual had reached physical maturity. In effect, the soul entered the body. Soul's presence on Earth increased, and the physical body vibrated at a faster rate. Unfortunately, the dramatic increase in the physical body's vibrational rate created much instability. The physical body popped out of the third dimension to return to a state of potential in the fourth and higher dimensions. Invoking spirit-light into the body during young adulthood made the body's vibration too high to be compatible with the physical plane. Invoking spirit-light worked, but it did not work well enough.

When the focus of experiments shifted to the use of the chakras to accommodate spirit, success followed. The creation of the chakra power centres predates the full descent into matter. At a time when human vibration stood at the edge of the doorway to the third dimension, the chakras worked to accept the higher frequencies already within the third dimension. The newly invented chakras held light, and the hope was that they might also hold the soul's spirit-light.

Essentially, the chakras worked, but could they accept frequencies from above the third dimension, and especially those of the soul? Full descent into matter immersed the chakras in the very slow vibrations of the physical plane and overwhelmed their ability to carry light. The chakras were able to manifest within the physical body, but were unable to function in the environment of Earth's density. They quickly fell into a state of dormancy. Dormant chakras were unprepared to accept spirit-light.

More than any other place in the body, the chakras accommo-

3 The term spirit-light refers to the light of the soul, and to the One-ness of the Soul. The Oneness or spirit-light is a tangible vibration that carries identity within the lighted universe. It is absolutely unique. In the eastern religions, soul Oneness, implanted in the base chakra, is called the kundalini or kundalini energies. The soul origin-ates within the heavens and extends its Oneness into the base chakra; it plants its "seed". Because of its starry origins and its seed-planting endeavours, another name for the Oneness of the soul is that of "star-seed". The use of the terms: starseed, spirit-light, Oneness of the soul, and kundalini, each refer to the very same energy.

dated the soul's spirit-light, but, because of the immediate problems that plagued progress, the innovation exercise had to be taken a step further. Invoking spirit-light into the adult body raised the body's vibration significantly, so high, in fact, that the body was unable to remain on Earth. The chakras accommodated light, yet too much light was getting into the body's essence. What to do?

As the experimentation process continued, light-workers perceived that using only one chakra might be the answer. When too much of the body was empowered with light, it became volatile and unstable in the third dimension. By empowering a lesser portion of the body, the problem might be alleviated. The base chakra was chosen, and further innovation followed.

The problem, most pertinent to implanting the high and subtle frequencies of spirit into the body's form, involved the need for compatible and manageable space. Spirit was a high vibration, but the body was a low vibration. Was compatibility possible? The option to lower the spirit's vibration was quickly rejected. Instead, the light-workers decided to raise the vibration of the physical body, especially the vibration of the base chakra, without destabilizing the body's third-dimensional vibration. Efforts then focussed on making the base chakra compatible with the soul.

Using the smaller base chakra, as compared to the larger body as-a-whole, provided a second advantage. That is, the process of invoking spirit into the body was scaled down. Less space and less light meant a less overwhelming and more manageable process. Further, because spirit entered the base chakra only, the body's vibration was unaffected and spirit did not pop out of the third dimension. The base chakra was therefore designed to serve as an incubator for the seed of the soul's spirit-light.

The light-workers had found the answers to the problems of anchoring the spirit-light of the soul, but not the key to conscious spiritual awakening. Chakra dormancy, caused by physical density, persisted. Spirit-light anchored within the base chakra, but had no where else to go. The base chakra remained as dormant as any other chakra. When love became part of the process of reproduction, the problem of dormancy and vibrational instability was resolved.

Love within the male raised the vibration of his impregnating sperm, and love within the female raised the vibration of her ovum. Even before conception, love worked to raise the vibration of each of the sexual partners. When their sperm and ovum united within the sanctity of love, the resulting fertilized egg vibrated faster as well. During the pregnancy, on-going love from the pregnant female and from the supporting male further cultivated the vibration of love within the growing embryo and fetus. Love raises the body's vibration (within man, woman, and fetus, both individually and as a family unit) to receive ever higher light frequencies. Within the sanctity of love, the heightened vibration of the base chakra easily received and maintained the seed-light of the soul.

At the moment of birth, the particular soul that incarnates into the newborn is determined by love. This is not to say that evolved souls are differentiated from unevolved souls and that only parents with higher love are blessed by a baby from a "better" soul. The quality of the soul is determined by a host of factors, foremost is the contractual arrangement made between the souls of the father, mother, and child. Differences in the quality and quantity of love contributed by the individual male or female for each other and their child-to-be, pose limits on the range of souls capable of entering the vibration emitted by a particular fetus. The outcome is not something over which the intellectual mind has any influence, except that the will to love raises the vibration within the fetal body.

Souls choose to incarnate to particular parents because those parents have the precise magnetically encoded configuration of vibration required to help the soul learn and progress as it needs to do. By raising the fetal vibration, the result is an expansion of the range of souls available to enter the baby's body at birth. Parental love sets up the fetus to receive the spirit-light of a soul having compatible qualities, but the choice to incarnate is the propriety of the soul and "compatibility" is defined by the heavens. Parental love, and especially the love given during the later stages of the pregnancy, creates the raised vibration needed to prepare the fetal body and its base chakra, but does not determine which soul comes to incarnate.

Love opens the base chakra to receive the spirit-light of the soul, and it also protects the soul's spirit after incarnating. The love vibrations of both the incoming seed-light and the fetal base chakra combine to spin a protective cocoon of love. The love cocoon becomes the space into which spirit-light enters; it surrounds and protects. The cocoon is made effective by its ability to ensure that only vibrations of love come in contact with the seed-light. Vibrations outside of love simply cannot penetrate the space within which spirit-light resides. And so, the essence of the base chakra, initially prepared by parental love, becomes the sacred temple that holds spirit in a state of dormancy until spirit opens to the outer world.

Love works to establish the vibration of the base chakra and to spin the protective cocoon. It also plays a role in future connections with the individual's heavenly soul. If the seed-light were able to connect continuously with its soul, the flow of light would not be limited. Unfortunately, the density of the third dimension poses a serious barrier that requires significant effort to overcome. Density often blocks the flow of light. It also inhibits the soul connection. The soul is unable to transfer any notable amount of light on an ongoing basis.

A second factor preventing the transfer of soul light is free-will. Until the individual is consciously and wilfully able to choose to work with his soul, the soul is obliged not to participate in its incarnation's life path. The love available at birth, the love provided by the parents during childhood, and the love encountered in the local environment all provide the foundation that sets up an individual's vibration to receive the presence of the soul. Any conscious aspiration toward love on the part of the growing child, at any time later in life, has the potential to attract the attention of the soul, and with it, divine light. Love is the essence of the heavens, and, when it pervades an individual's vibration on Earth, heaven and Earth unite.

By implanting the seed-light of the soul into the base chakra, the angelic light-workers had achieved the innovation needed to circumvent the problem of Earthly density. The seed-light brought a small, and therefore, manageable amount of the soul's presence into a small physical space. Overwhelming soul light was not forced to return to the higher dimensions; and overwhelming physical density did not prevent the presence of the soul from remaining on Earth. The presence of the soul on Earth, however, was a mere wisp of the larger soul. If the soul was to continue to flourish on the physical plane, the delicate seed-light would have to be nurtured with great care, much love, and the blessings of divine grace.

3.5 Awakening the Seed-Light

One small step for seed-light, one giant leap for Earth.
Seed-light has landed. All systems are . . . dormant?

If the problem of bringing the soul's seed-light into the base chakra was not enough, the next problem was releasing it.

By the time the innovations to make the base chakra fully functional were complete, the human body was constructed with the seven-chakra system familiar in today's world. Form of any kind manifests itself into the lower heavens, and into the third dimension in particular, without light. The chakras are no different. They too, manifested only to await the arrival of light frequencies as they became available. Without light, all seven chakras and their connecting pathways existed in dormancy within the human body from the moment of birth. Empowering the chakras with light, starting with the base chakra, leads to their opening and to spiritual awakening.

Through its seed-light, the soul had extended itself onto Earth, but sat cloistered and dormant. The extreme density of the physical plane reinforced the need for all of the innovations using love and the base chakra for protection. But isolated by the love cocoon and hidden deep within the base chakra, the soul's seed-light was unable to connect with the outside world. All of its codes, prescribing life on Earth, remained hidden away. The important information they carried was pivotal to every lesson and to every influence guiding the individual's life path. If life on Earth was to have meaning, the dormant seed-light had to be released.

The seed-light had come from love in the heavens, and had imbibed itself into the love cocoon in the base chakra. If the seed-light was to break out of the base chakra and expand into physical vibration, love had to lead the way.

The contribution of the love cocoon was crucial. It prevented vibrations outside of love from resonating with the base chakra. Only love—and nothing but love—was able to pierce through the many protective layers that encased the seed-light. These layers provided fortification to the base chakra and made it impossible for all but the strongest vibrations of love to have any influence. The base chakra did not open and the seed-light of the soul was not released until love dissolved the protective layers of the love cocoon.

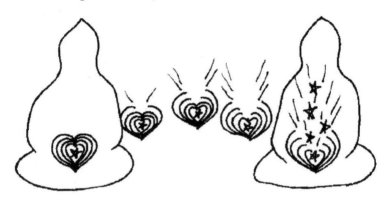

In the presence of love, the protective love cocoon opens to release the starseed of the soul.

The opening of the base chakra and the release of the soul's seed-light is essentially the spiritual awakening. It is the raising of the kundalini and the beginning of the spiritual path. Because only love can unlock the doorway to the seed-light held by the love cocoon, only love can bring an individual forward to the spiritual path. The wisdom of the heavens has created the checks and balances that ensure that the spiritual path on Earth begins only with love.

The love needed to open the base chakra comes primarily from external sources, and can also come from within. In the earliest times on Earth, love from within was of greater importance because the love from external sources was nearly non-existent. Few frequencies were able to resonate with the Earth's density; and few were able to penetrate the Earth's etherics. Recognizing the problem, the most powerful of the Earth's light-workers took incarnate form with the intent of opening the base chakra using their own love. By generating enough love from within their incarnate forms, the adept light-worker was able to open his base chakra.

Hallelujah!

The task was not accomplished in those early times in a single incarnation. Much had to be learned first. Step-by-step instructions were not available to guide light-workers who sought to open their base chakras. In most instances, an individual's memory about his original purpose was erased once he entered Earth's density. The task was understood in the heavens by those discarnate light-workers who looked on, but what could be done on Earth? Try and try again? Although the obstacles were many, the will to create the needed love from within was strong enough to prevail. Spiritual awakenings followed.

As love alone was the way, light-workers intent on opening their base chakras, used whatever means worked. They incarnated into places where light was abundant. They lived in the Earth's power spots and light vortexes. They gravitated toward sedentary life-styles to maintain themselves in a state of peace and tranquillity. They avoided situations of turbulence and disturbance. Through isolation from other vibrations, the love created from within their own bodies on Earth had a chance to grow. When the love within was strong enough, the base chakra opened, and the seed-light of the soul spilled out.

As time on Earth passed, the importance to the spiritual awakening of love from external sources increased. Love from another light-worker was first among those external forces able to open the base chakra.

Any light-worker, intent on helping others with their spiritual awakenings, must first himself be fully awake. If an incarnate light-worker has created enough love within his own body to open his own base chakra and initiate his own spiritual journey, the journey itself will continue until he reaches enlightenment. Thereafter, enlighten-ment and the steps beyond enlightenment will solidify the incarnate person's connection with his soul. When a soul and its incarnation are so divinely aligned as to be enlightened, love from the higher planes flows freely. The enlightened incarnation is then vested with the power to channel heavenly love into the base chakra of other in-dividuals to contribute to their chakras' openings and spiritual awak-enings. In honour of the Pact of One, many adept light-workers vol-unteered to return to Earth to help others awaken.

A second external source of love, capable of opening the base chakra, is the Earth. Because black light frequencies are indigenous to both the Earth and the base chakra, the Earth's light and love res-onate directly with the base chakra. Earth's light can pierce through the protective cocoon's layers of love to open it and enter. Spiritual awakenings involving the Earth take place among individuals who are well grounded in a solitary existence. In our urban society, indi-viduals who are drawn to "go back to the land" are simply following the attraction of the love of the planet playing upon the base chakra. The nurturing quality of Mother Earth becomes their experience as the awakening to spirit takes its most natural course.

A third external means to open the base chakra is a crystal—Smoky Quartz. Smoky Quartz[4] carries both the white-light frequen-cies of the I AM presence within its original clear quartz compon-

---

4 Smoky Quartz is naturally radiated by the black light frequencies that originate directly from the original source of all creation in the Godhead. At times, the Godhead emits black light intended spe-cifically for Earth. The black frequencies are taken in by the Earth's etherics and routed throughout the planet to wherever they are need-ed. To create Smoky Quartz, the angelic light-workers orchestrate a hole or opening in the Earth's etherics over a deposit of clear quartz. The hole permits the Godhead's black frequencies to descend directly onto the deposit, thereby causing the radiation of the clear quartz into Smoky Quartz.

ent and the black-light frequencies of the Earth within its radiated component. The base chakra also carries the same white and black frequencies. In the base chakra, white light is the essence of the seed-light of the soul, and black light is the grounding frequency of the Earth imbibed within the chakra's essence-form. Because they have the same frequencies in common, Smoky Quartz and the base chakra share a profound harmony.

In every other instance, opening the base chakra comes through love, not through frequencies of light. Love is the key to the opening, after which light enters. Frequencies of light vibrate at their own frequency rate different from the frequency rate of the base chakra, except for Smoky Quartz. Smoky Quartz is the exception because no other medium or crystal carries the exact frequencies needed to work with the base chakra to initiate the spiritual awakening. As the base chakra and Smoky Quartz share identical frequencies, there is no resistance to their exchange of light. Smoky Quartz is the crystal of spiritual initiation[5].

Smoky Quartz does not break through the layers of the protective love cocoon in the same way as love from external sources. Rather, light frequencies from Smoky Quartz merge with the essence of the base chakra. The crystal creates an osmotic flow of light to and from the seed-light. There is no dramatic penetration of the chakra, and therefore, no definitive opening. Upon using Smoky Quartz, light moves gently into the base chakra, gradually exposing it to ex-

---

5 IMPORTANT CAUTION: Smoky Quartz is the stone of initiation, but can be copied artificially by radiating clear quartz. The artificially radiated stone may have noticeable dark bands or veins, but can also be very difficult to distinguish from natural Smoky Quartz. A Smoky Quartz that is very dark and comes from the commercial marketplace is almost always an artificial specimen. Artificial Smoky Quartz resonates with the base chakra, as does the natural specimen, but does not carry the divine vibrations of the Godhead. It has no love. The fake piece causes etheric distortions and chakra damage that may take multiple lifetimes to correct. Upon discovering an artificially radiated Smoky Quartz, your only option is to place it in the trash. To give it away to someone is to create unwanted karma.

ternal light. The result is an interface between the base chakra and its external environment. Through the interface, light moves into the chakra causing it to open.

A final means to initiate the spiritual path is through love itself. Because love opens the base chakra, any source of love will contribute. Your marriage partner, your children, your father, yourself, the neighbours, good friends, and friendly letter-carriers qualify. Your dog, your cat, the animals of the forest, the trees, the crystals, and your flower garden all provide love that contributes to the raising of vibration and to the spiritual awakening that follows. Anyone and anything that exists within love's vibration supports the opening of the base chakra. The degree to which they are a factor is dependent upon the strength of their love.

The grace of love ensures that the base chakra of the spiritual adherent opens in a gentle manner when he is ready. The opening can also be quite dramatic. If the body is unprepared, if its vibration is too low, it will be unable to handle the surge of high and subtle soul frequencies caused by the release of the seed-light. The surge, moving upward in a body full of density and blockages, causes imbalances that can become serious. Opening the base chakra too quickly creates the risk of physical body damage that can develop into dis-ease, both temporary and permanent, as well as possible mental insanity. Both body and mind can be destabilized by the radical shift in the light energies to which they are exposed.

In contrast, the spiritual devotee, who has participated in the disciplines of meditation, prayer, and chanting, or has otherwise raised his vibration sufficiently, is prepared and in harmony with his soul. His body's vibration merges with the surging seed-light without resistance. Problems are easily avoided if the devotee trusts his own intuitive sense about what feels right and pursues his spiritual growth at his own pace.

Love is the way and the light. Love prepares the way for spirit to enter the physical plane; love is the key that unlocks the door to the seed-light of the soul; and love allows the spiritual journey on Earth to begin.

3.6 Getting Off to a Good Start

Break out the champagne! The base chakra is open and the energies of the soul are rising. Cut the ribbon! The spiritual path has officially begun!

When the base chakra opens, the seed-light of the soul emerges from its state of dormancy. It enters and interacts with the vibrations of the third dimension. The cocoon opens; life is released. Finally, spirit dwells on Earth.

The opening of the base chakra represents the soul's precarious toe-hold on third-dimensional vibration. It marks the very beginning of an individual's spiritual life, meaning that the journey is ahead with very little behind. Having an opened base chakra, the devotee can look forward to developing the disciplines of spiritual life and the effort it takes to achieve enlightenment. It is a journey. She becomes a traveller wandering through time and space, acquiring light frequencies here and more light frequencies there. At journey's end, she becomes enlightened. The emergence of the soul's seed-light from the base chakra is the spiritual awakening and defines the start of the spiritual path.

The spiritual journey is indigenous to Earth. In the heavens, spirit is all around and all encompassing. There is no need to journey anywhere or do anything. Enlightenment in the heavens is a constant state of being. On Earth our task involves bringing enough light onto the physical plane to anchor and fully connect the physical body with the higher-self. We are here to enlighten ourselves and our world.

The journey to enlightenment begins with the opening of the base chakra. It has a beginning, and, like any other vibration caught in Earth's time and space continuum, it has an end. With the achievement of the enlightened state, an individual no longer needs to travel the spiritual path. She has arrived; she has imbibed the presence of her heavenly self on Earth. The spiritual journey, which only happens on Earth, begins in the unenlightened state and ends with enlightenment.

The path to enlightenment has no shortcuts; all that needs to be done will be done first. In centuries past, the journey to enlightenment took many lifetimes and was unattainable for most people. In the very beginning, merely stabilizing the seed-light of the soul was a monumental accomplishment. The beginning, however, was a long time ago. We are now fully immersed in the flood of light frequencies bathing the Earth. We have entered the dawning of the Age of Aquarius, and with it comes great promise and great abundance of light.

The spiritual journey itself has not changed. Each step in the unfolding new era is the same as each step has always been. Although there has never been more than one path, the difference between the past and now is the difference between walking in the black of night and walking in the brilliance of broad daylight. In the past, the devotee had to crawl, feeling her way in the dark. But the dark ages are past. Now, all on the spiritual path is illuminated. The devotee can get up and run with certainty about what lies ahead and where the path leads. What took lifetimes, now takes years and months. Never before on Earth has there been the great abundance of light, nor the high quality of light now available. With more light, the spiritual journey has not changed, but it has picked up considerable speed.

Step one on the spiritual path is the opening of the base chakra and the release of the soul's Oneness. Step two is the awakening and opening of the body's other chakras.

Throughout most of our time on Earth, the design of the human body has included seven major chakras and a few connecting pathways that form the chakra distribution system[6]. In the very first experiments with body design, light-workers created a three-chakra system with no connecting pathways. In subsequent experiments, bodies were designed with successively more chakras until the opti-

---

6 In Sanskrit, the chakras include: Sahasrara (crown), Ajna (third eye), Vishuddha (throat), Anahata (heart), Manipura (solar plexus or navel), Swadhisthana (sacral or pelvic), and Muladhara (base) chakras, and the connecting pathways are called the Ida, Pingala, and Shushumna.

mum number was realized. Some bodies came to Earth with up to three dozen, but it was soon discovered that seven was adequate. A few of Earth's light-workers may count the hands and feet and other places in the body as chakras, but the major chakras include the crown, third eye, throat, heart, navel, pelvic, and base chakras. They are interconnected by the pathways of the chakra distribution system, which runs up the centre of the spine and in spirals along each side.

Throughout eons of time, seven chakras[7] have served well in the quest to bring the physical body into a state of enlightenment. Yet the dawning new age brings some changes. The concerns of the past focussed on the anchoring of light into the physical body. In the new age, the focus has shifted to the use of the human body as a bridge between the Earth and heaven. Therefore, chakras have been added. There are three more upper chakras to connect the physical being to the universal mind, the light-body, and the cosmic beyond, as well as an Earth chakra to complete the bridging function to the physical plane. Although the more recent changes hold great interest, the original seven chakras need to be understood first.

Regardless of which chakra system is in fashion, step two of the spiritual journey involves using the seed-light of the base chakra to open the upper chakras. In the eastern religions, the process is called raising the kundalini. The kundalini, symbolized by a serpent, uncoils from around the base chakra and rises to open the upper chakras. In more familiar language, the seed-light of the soul germinates when nurtured by love, grows out of its protective cocoon, and radiates forth to open the upper chakras. The upper chakras come out of their state of dormancy at the moment the seed-light touches their essence-form.

One of the many innovations created to protect the seed-light ensures that the upper chakras open only to the seed-light of the soul,

---

7 Each chakra works with a set range of light frequencies. The body needs the primary frequencies to be empowered, but does not need to be cluttered with a host of secondary frequencies that contribute only marginally. The seven chakra system was more than adequate to deliver the primary frequencies. Extra chakras were simply unnecessary.

and further, only to the seed-light occupying the base chakra. Potentially, light from other souls can affect the dormant upper chakras and gain a hold within the body. But two souls contending for the same body create unacceptable havoc. Each has its own personality, or even multiple personalities, to impose upon the incarnation. The resulting chaos was not what the creator of humanity intended.

Keeping the problem of intruding souls in check necessitated another innovation. The first line of defence against unwanted light of any kind is the etheric body. Although the high and subtle vibrations of intruding souls are not subjected to etheric magnetism, the solution was still to be found in the encoding of the etherics.

Even though the seed-light's presence is reflected in the configuration of the etheric field, it remained dormant and concealed, lending no energy to empower the field's filtering mechanisms. The unempowered etheric body was defenceless against the energy of an intruding soul. How could the person's etheric body be reconfigured and strengthened enough to deal with unwanted souls, without disturbing the dormant seed-light?

Once again, the base chakra provided the answer. It already housed the incubating seed-light and grounded frequencies indigenous to the Earth. A further modification to its essence allowed it to reflect the same vibrations found in the body as-a-whole. The vibration of the modified base chakra then became identical to the person's overall vibration. In turn, the base chakra's etheric magnet field became identical to the individual's overall etheric magnetic field.

The mix of energies of the incarnate body became part of the vibration of the base chakra. But more important, the mix of energies of the base chakra become part of the vibration of the incarnate body. As a result, the presence of the seed-light in the base chakra was automatically reflected in the etheric bodies of both the base chakra and the body as-a-whole. Without bringing the soul's seed-light out of dormancy, this innovation allowed the etheric codes of the base chakra, including the codes of the soul, to be amplified throughout the incarnate body's etheric field. Vibrational compatibility, between the body and the soul, was then only possible with the seed-light of the soul that already occupied the base chakra. The etheric field configuration repelled any unwanted soul energies. As a result, there can be no mistake about which soul's seed-light opens the upper chakras.

Step one: opening the base chakra, and step two: opening the six upper chakras mark the very beginning of the spiritual journey. These are baby's first steps. The innovation developed to prevent the intrusion of unwanted and potentially mischievous souls allowed the incarnate life-path to stay on track. Rearranging the etheric body to reflect the individual's vibration as-a-whole, including the vibration of the soul's seed-light, enabled the incarnate being to get off to a good start.

3.7 Chakra Empowerment

The process of empowering the six upper chakras is easy enough to understand. Light frequencies passing into the chakra-distribution system are attracted by the particular chakra with which they resonate. The chakra then assimilates those frequencies it needs for empowerment. As light combines with the essence of the chakra's manifest-form, the chakra then becomes Oneness. As Oneness, its work begins. The empowerment of the chakras takes time, often lifetimes, because there are problems along the way.

The first prerequisite for empowering the chakras is that they be opened; the second prerequisite is that they receive the light needed.

To receive light, light must first be available. On Earth, availability has been a chronic problem. Any light coming to Earth passes through the etheric filter. If a light frequency is not within an acceptable range, either too high and subtle or too low and dense, the etheric magnetic field blocks its entry, thus preventing its availability.

During the early days of time on Earth, the range of acceptable frequencies was extremely limited. Expanding the range was a painstakingly slow process. Earth's own vibration had to rise if more light was to be attracted to it. Until the Earth had evolved further, the quality and quantity of light needed to empower the chakras was unable to pass through the planet's etheric field. The first problem that related to the empowerment of the chakras, is simple to understand: without the necessary light frequencies, empowerment does not begin.

In the higher realms, light frequencies exist in a state of wholeness and completeness. They are comprised of parts that belong to different dimensions including a third-dimensional component in potential form. When a potential light frequency descends to Earth, its third-dimensional component is realized as physical vibration. But its higher dimensional component remains in the higher dimensions. Only that portion of the frequency capable of entering physical density comes to the Earth's surface. Many of the frequencies and many of the parts of frequencies available to Earth were too high to cross the threshold into physical density, and so, remained unavailable for chakra empowerment. The etheric body of the Earth blocked some of the incoming frequencies, and it blocked mere portions of the incoming frequencies as well.

Once the appropriate range of light frequencies became available, the problem shifted to the ability of the chakras to open and receive. When physical form descends to Earth, it manifests as much of its vibration as possible. However, some of form's potentials are too high to descend into the extreme density of the third dimension. In the same way as the higher aspects of light are unable to manifest on Earth, the higher and more subtle aspects of form are also unable to manifest. Much of form's potential remained in the heavens—unavailable. Because only form's slower and more basic aspects make their way onto the physical plane, only slower and more basic light frequencies can be assimilated.

The problems of descending onto the physical plane are the same for any manifest form including the chakras. The higher aspects of the chakras' forms split away from the lower and slower aspects and remained in the heavens. Only the slower and more basic aspects, which could adapt to physical density, descend to Earth to become available for the work of assimilating light. This means that the chakras' ability to empower the physical body with light is restricted to slower and more basic light frequencies. Only the basic frequencies are compatible. Over time, however, ever higher aspects of form's potentials descended onto the Earth. With higher vibrational form, more and higher light frequencies are assimilated; and the limitations to the process of empowerment are overcome.

The empowerment of the chakras begins with the opening of its light receptors. From the light flowing through the chakra distribution system, each light receptor picks up the one and only light frequency with which it resonates and transfers the frequency to the chakra. Among the chakra's light-receptors are different receptors for both higher and lower frequencies. When the chakra first emerges from dormancy, only the lower frequency receptors are functional. When initially empowered, the chakra opens and assimilates light, but most of its receptors remain shrouded in darkness. The lowest and most basic receptor emerges first.

The order in which frequencies are assimilated is absolutely precise. Only after the lowest functional receptor has assimilated the one unique frequency, with which it resonates, can the next higher receptor open. The lowest receptor and its specific frequency combine to become Oneness, which in turn raises the vibration of the immediate area enough to open the next higher receptor. If the next needed frequency is unavailable, the chakra's vibration remains the same and evolution has to wait. But if the next needed frequency is available, light combines with form and Oneness expands within the chakra—one frequency at-a-time, and one light-receptor at-a-time. The sequence is in perfect order. It progresses only as fast as light becomes available and receptors open.

Because chakra empowerment depends upon available light, the soul works to ensure that its incarnation is exposed to the frequencies that best serve the enlightenment process. Geography plays a part. In any one location on the planet, some frequencies are in greater abundance than others. Souls therefore incarnate into locations that have an abundance of the light needed to fulfill their particular purposes. If a certain area carries the light needed for emerging souls, individuals found in that area will generally be the incarnations of emerging souls. Similarly, a geographical location having the frequencies needed by young souls will attract the incarnations of young souls. Souls direct their incarnate forms to the geographical area having the light frequencies that are most favourable to chakra empowerment.

Because over time the person will assimilate most or all of the light frequencies available from any one geographical area, he will need new frequencies to continue the evolutionary march towards enlightenment. If the individual remains in the same location with exposure only to the frequencies immediately available, spiritual growth soon stagnates. To avoid such problems, the growing soul, with or without the conscious involvement of the person, directs its incarnation to relocate. Sometimes growth means living where the sun shines every day of the year. Sometimes growth means living beside a deposit of copper or gold. Sometimes growth means experiencing the balance of winter and summer seasons. Each of us lives where we do because home possesses the light we need for our own personal empowerment. When the frequencies available to enhance empowerment are exhausted, our soul helps to create the circumstances that move us to another location having the light we need for the next step on our spiritual journey.

In today's world, the availability of easy long-distance travel (cars, trains, aeroplanes) allows individuals to commute to places where frequencies needed for growth can be found. The summer vacation to the cottage is often for the purpose of creating the quiet environment needed to assimilate light. The business trip to the Virgin Islands may serve the purpose of direct exposure to the sun's rays. On a more local level, a trip to the park can put us in a place of calm where we are better able to assimilate light and where light vibrations tend to be higher. Convenient travel access to places having new and needed frequencies for growth is a manifestation of how the spiritual path has accelerated in our current age.

As the person matures by accumulating a greater variety and a wider range of light frequencies, the options about where to incarnate increase. The incarnation of an evolved soul has numerous options and does not need to be concerned about "prerequisite" frequencies needed for priority experiences. The evolved soul has already completed the required lessons, and can therefore go where it chooses for its spiritual growth. Having the mobility and option to travel to places where specialized frequencies can be readily acquired speeds the journey towards enlightenment.

The steps a person takes, even in his daily life, are very often directed by the soul seeking the light frequencies needed for incarnate empowerment. If the individual and his soul are well connected, empowerment accelerates considerably. The soul is then able to send light directly to the incarnation for assimilation and the enhancement of incarnate Oneness. In turn, the enhanced Oneness further enhances the ability of the soul to connect with its incarnation. As light begets more light with each new opening and each expansion of Oneness, empowerment accelerates.

3.8 Choosing the Spiritual Path

3.8.1 The Perils of the Path

The spiritual path is like the winding mountain road. The road twists and curves; its surface is bumpy and uneven; it can wash away in places making it impassable; and it has numerous hair-pin turns, any one of which can cause disastrous results. Its challenges invoke fear, and each step needs to be taken with care.

Both being on the spiritual path and climbing the mountain road are uphill endeavours. The exhausting difficulty of the climb ensures that each step is made with certainty of focus. Because upward progress is slow, the traveller has plenty of time to negotiate the path and all of its dangers without yielding to fear. Climbing the mountain is a matter of steady determination and the expressed discipline needed to put one foot carefully ahead of the other. Being on the spiritual path also takes discipline. Each step is a lesson in life whereby the individual assimilates one light frequency after another. The spiritual journey and the mountain road are indeed similar— both take effort to get to the top.

If a person pictures herself on the winding mountain road on the way to spiritual enlightenment, she may consider the situation as it has been for most of the past. The Earth began its sojourn into the third dimension immersed in the blackness of the void. Light was absent. We learned to contend with the darkness of the darkest ages. In effect, we have been finding our way through the night. Seeing the next step has not always been possible. Humanity has had to get down on its hands and knees to feel its way towards enlightenment. In literally feeling our way, feelings have played a major role! What feels right and what feels wrong have been important signposts in deciding which directions to take in the ascension toward higher vibration and love. Humanity initially found its way to its spiritual awakening, not by walking the spiritual path, but by crawling and feeling the way.

Once the climb up the mountain is complete, the vision and landscape of the spiritual path are clear to see. What brings us to the heights of vibration where love is abundant enough to open the base chakra and release the Oneness of the soul?

3.8.2 Free-Choice by Design

In the beginning, the concerted effort of a significant number of light-workers was sometimes not enough to bring about spiritual awakening. Teams of angels working with groups of the most evolved of Earth's light-workers took great pains to work out the steps to open the base chakra. But the spiritual journey had to be made accessible to all. How does the simple devotee find her way?

The answer is free choice. Every choice counts!

The spiritual seeker may or may not be consciously aware of the significance of what she is doing, but choices made in daily life determine where she goes. God created the Earth as a free-will zone. We can choose or not choose the spiritual path. To enter the spiritual path, free-will needs to be expressed. Because only love opens the base chakra releasing the soul's seed-light, the seeker must freely choose love before the spiritual path can begin.

Whenever a person chooses directions in life that lead towards spiritual awakening, her vibration automatically rises. Choices that raise vibration and accelerate spiritual growth are more attractive because they simply feel better. The higher vibration of enlightened living is dis-synchronous with the lower vibration of unenlightened living. The individual will feel out-of-place with any negativity encountered. As she becomes sensitive to negativity, she acquires a tendency to actively reject its place in her daily life. At the same time as positive choices feel better, negative choices feel worse. By choosing to live in the right way, the individual creates a pattern of living that leads to ever higher vibration.

The analogy of climbing the mountain serves to further illustrate the point. Choosing love begins at the bottom of the mountain where the view of the path ahead is obscured. Not only is the peak not within the line of sight, seeing past the rocks and bushes close-at-hand presents its own difficulty. To get anywhere, the path leads upward. Similarly, the spiritual seeker's choices must take her to places of raised vibration. On Sunday morning, the choice to attend church raises the vibration much more than the choice to go to the horse races. The choice to be kind to those we find annoying raises the vibration much more than the choice to blurt out harsh judgements. If we choose to act right, eat right, think right, and go to the right places[8], at the same time as we move away from places of avarice, deceit, or drunkenness, we allow ourselves to walk with raised vibrations. Although understanding why we do what we do is not essential, choosing love takes us out of the obscurity of darkness and ever upward towards spiritual fulfilment.

If you find yourself attempting to climb the mountain of spiritual growth in the middle of the night with darkness all around, ask yourself: "Does this feel like I'm going up?" In other words, the first steps of the spiritual seeker may be made in a state of blind anticipation with very little understanding of what to do or where to go. Fear not, my friend, the angels are awaiting your arrival, but they cannot interfere with the means you choose to express your free choice and to grow in spirit. Do your choices feel right for you?

In the period prior to the start of the spiritual path, there are no dramas. Progressive choices are absolutely simple, mundane, and quite grounded. They include, for example, choosing a better diet, choosing to attend meditation classes, choosing to mow the neighbour's lawn, choosing to thank the waitress for her service, choosing to help the kids with their homework, and choosing to buy a pair of shoes that simply make you "feel good". Each individual choice brings you closer to the spiritual path whenever it serves to raise your vibration.

Sniffed any flowers lately?

God's will determined that Earth be a free-will zone, and so, the choice to walk the spiritual path must be made freely. Influences from the higher-self or our guardian angels violate the edict of free-will. To be valid, choices must come from within ourselves and from an Earthly level.

How can our choices be free on Earth when our very existence is divinely inspired? How could a choice be separated from the influence of the heavenly planes to be truly of the Earth?

---

8 The rights mentioned are loosely associated with the Eight-Fold Path of Buddhism. The eight rights of this path are right understanding, right intention, right speech, right action, right livelihood, right effort, right mindfulness, and right concentration.

Enter the intellect. Logical thought, calculated rationale, analysis, and the process of elimination arise from the intellect. More important, they arise strictly from within the Earth's third dimension. A choice based on logic qualifies as a choice arising strictly from within our free-will zone. A thoughtful analysis of the pros and cons, before making a decision to practice meditation, qualifies as a choice made within our free-will zone. Because the intellect is operated exclusively by the mind on Earth, any choice inspired by the intellect cannot be influenced by the higher realms, and is, therefore, truly free. Responsibility for the free-will decision to awaken spiritually has, therefore, been made the propriety of the intellect.

Using the intellect to choose the spiritual path is not divinely inspired and may not appear to be of any consequence, but it clearly demonstrates our true will on Earth to the heavenly hosts, if not to ourselves. Through the intellect, we create a pattern of choices that determine the directions we take in life. Here is where the "rights" of our choices demonstrate our love. An individual chooses peace over war. She chooses to be nice to a friend, to buy flowers for her mother, to pet the neighbour's dog, to be fair with her employees, to put her litter in the trash bin, and to be courteous while driving. Each of the examples falls within the aegis of the intellect without the help of divine inspiration, and is, therefore, a free choice. If an individual makes mindful, positive, and right-thinking choices one-after-another, she demonstrates a pattern that communicates the quality of her love. When the pattern of free choices has generated enough steps toward love, the potential to open the base chakra can be realized.

The logical mind requires no conscious connection with the higher-self, but it can generate the vibration of love within us needed to go farther. The mind, through its use of the intellect, is most capable of discerning what illusions it faces. The intellect is not attuned to the wisdom of the ancients, but it does allow an individual to eliminate rationally the problems of the third dimension that are inconsistent with love.

However, beyond accentuating the positive and eliminating the negative, the intellect is unable to take the enlightenment process any farther. The intellect is limited to third-dimensional insight. Because it is limited to the third dimension, it holds the key for choosing freely to step onto the spiritual path. It creates the foundation of positive free choices upon which our own personal vibration of love rests. The intellect is the launching pad for spiritual growth.

3.9 Connecting with Soul

The intellect is only one side of the human mind. The other side is the intuition. Through the intellect, the mind connects with the physical world; through the intuition, the mind connects with the enlightened universe.

The intuitive side of the mind opens our worldly viewpoint to the possibilities beyond the third dimension. Through intuition, a person is able to connect with his soul, as well as the unlimited Oneness of the lighted universe. Through the intuition's interface with heavenly Oneness, all light from all dimensions and everything that creation has to offer becomes available.

As the advocates of positive thinking often assert, our potential is only limited by our mind. With access to all of the light frequencies of the heavens, the mind is only limited by its own ability to receive. Indeed, the intuitive mind is the individual's doorway to the heavens; but more importantly, it is the soul's doorway to the individual. The mind is the bridge for consciousness flowing between Earth and heaven.

When the individual's mindful connection between heaven and Earth is stable and open, the soul participates in the activities of living on Earth. It sends and receives the light frequencies through which it orchestrates the directions of the incarnate life. If the mind is clear, and access to the heavens is strong, all of the light frequencies in creation become available through the soul, and therefore, all potential on Earth can be realized.

Without the need for a person's consciousness or even awareness, soul-sent light frequencies set up the etheric magnetic field to attract and repel light from the local environment, as well as from situations and events. But if the intuitive mind of the person is unable to interface with the heavens, the soul can watch its incarnation on Earth, and nothing more.

Interventions of the soul rarely violate free-will. The soul takes its lead from the individual. It facilitates the individual's choices, good or bad, without judgement. Whenever the individual expresses a will to choose, the soul does its best to help. If the individual repeatedly affirms that he is having a good day and the connection with his soul is strong enough, the soul will send the appropriate light frequencies to fulfill the free-will to have a good day. Conversely, if he so chooses, a connected soul is also able to help a person to have a 'bad' day[9]. To the soul, all experiences, good and bad, are beneficial to its evolution.

The role of the soul has another side. It sends light frequencies to help the individual acquire the experiences he wants according to his free will. The soul, however, does not subscribe to the illusions or denials influencing its incarnation. It sees what the individual wants in truth. The lung cancer patient may say he wants to be healed, but in truth, he expresses the will, consciously or unconsciously, to be self-destructive by continuing to smoke. The soul is not likely to help him to be self-destructive, but until he stops his self-destructive behaviour, the soul cannot violate his true free-will by helping him to heal. Although the soul facilitates the experiences that are wanted, what a person professes he wants does not always pass the test of truth.

The individual receives his life-experiences as a function of perception. The soul orchestrates an individual's personal experiences by sending the light frequencies needed to create his free-will choices. How will the experience be perceived once it manifests into reality? Again, free-will takes precedence, making a person free to

---

9 The angelic realms do not judge 'good' or 'bad' as humanity might see the conduct of life. As long as 'bad' does not impose destructive outcomes upon self or others, the angels and higher-self are free to help fulfill the will. Where destructive outcomes are intended, such as effecting revenge, the angelic realms and higher-self simply do not participate. Their response is no response. They do not even chastise.

choose whatever perception he wants.

Perception is key to shaping the directions of our lives. When the soul creates an experience in accordance with the person's true free-will, he is free to perceive the experience as good or bad or anything in-between. The experience is sent by the soul, and therefore, oozes with divine light. If he is determined to see the experience as a burden and negative, the flow of his energies and life directions will take the path toward negative outcomes. Thereafter, the downward slide gains speed. The negative directions that a person's life takes are a function of his negative perceptions. In the same situation, the same individual can instead choose to see the divinity that lies behind each and every experience. To search for the deeper meaning in life is to see and accept all that is divinely positive and to use it to create life's directions in cooperation with the soul.

Will a person see the divine light through the illusions? Can he see the positive grace inherent to every experience?

Because the soul is responsible for sending the light to enhance our choices, our experiences are always divinely coordinated. If a person is unable to see or feel divinity intuitively, the mind's other side, the intellect, can be used to create a foundation of logical thought to bring a person out of illusion and into the divine.

Using logic: the soul sends light; light is divine; light generates experience; experience comes from light. Conclusion: experience is divinely created by the soul.

The intellect helps to create logical understanding, and can be used to interpret experience. It soon exposes misperceptions and illusions for what they are. It can add one truth to another truth to synthesize what is not immediately apparent. The intellect can show us that the illusions in our lives are not founded in truth, and therefore have no strength or substance. Illusions do not add up; they cannot pass even the lowly test of logic. The intellect can help us to see that every experience has divine love at its core.

On the side opposite to negative perceptions and well beyond the illusions, rational thought, logic, calculation, and analysis are the tools of the intellectual mind that work to bring about positive perceptions. When positive perceptions are chosen, our lives take positive directions. When divine perceptions are chosen, our lives take divine directions. When positive and divine perceptions are chosen over illusions and negative perceptions, our lives take us where vibration rises and love is abundant.

If you are "having one of those days", do you perceive the day to be positive? Or negative? Where will a positive perception lead? Where will a negative perception lead?

The intellect helps the mind to harmonize with the physical plane to create positive perceptions. The higher vibration of a positive-thinking mind creates the compatibility with the soul needed to solidify the mind-soul connection.

When an individual accepts the role of the intellect and rational thinking and intuitively perceives the divinity behind every experience, his vibration rises. His raised vibration generates a deeper and more profound connection with the soul and attracts higher and more subtle light frequencies.

3.10 Love's Role in Free choice

Getting started on the spiritual path requires that the aspiring individual choose love to enable the process of opening the base chakra. The alternative is not to choose love and to remain engrossed in slower and denser vibration. Although we have free choice on

Earth, only love leads to spiritual growth.

The angels and discarnate light-workers who reside in the higher dimensions are beyond concerns with free-will. Their real choice amounts to choosing one manifestation of love or another manifestation of love. Because the heavens exist in a state of total love, choosing anything outside of love is impossible. Even if a higher dimensional being chooses to incarnate into a lower plane outside the love of the lighted universe, the choice to do so is based on her will to extend love into the lower plane. The choice in the heavens is freely made, but always comes from love and goes to love, never leaving the bounds of love.

In contrast, persons on Earth are not surrounded by love, and so, possible choices include both love and what lies outside of love. Humanity is surrounded by duality. Our choices involve the negative polarity, the positive polarity, any union of the two, or nothing at all. We can choose from good or bad, left or right, proficiency or procrastination, love or hate, and any other number of opposites. Because not all on Earth is love, choosing love cannot be taken for granted.

The incarnate light-worker comes to Earth with numerous illusions that block her connection with her higher-self. She also comes without memories about her origins in the heavens. The difficulties created by dense physical vibration result in profound separation from the truth. Choices made often arise from fear, repression, denial, disrespect, and other negative aspects of duality. Life on Earth is full of deviations from love's ways. As a result, Earth's light-workers do not always choose love when exercising free-will.

Making choices leads us through life and its outcomes. When choices take us away from love, we arrive in unloving places. The problems created by density on the physical plane are more than abundant. Murder, war, rape, and violence are hardly on love's side of duality's equation, but they are part of the human experience. Our true nature is love; our mission on Earth is love; the spiritual path is carpeted with love; but we are not obligated to choose love because we have free-will within the duality of choices. We are free to choose outside of love's vibration. However, choices come with built-in consequences. Unloving choices attract karmic lessons and lower our vibration.

When a person chooses against love, she chooses against herself. The descent to Earth and into third-dimensional density results from our will in the heavens to participate in God's great mission on Earth. Each of us arrives fully encoded with our agenda of lessons and our purpose to carry out the will of God. Our entire vibration is the extension of our heavenly soul's divinity onto the Earth. Because all of manifest creation springs forth from the divine Godhead, all creation is love at its core. The nature of our being-ness is love. To choose to be is to choose to be love, which defines our true nature. If we fail to choose love, we move away from higher purpose, away from our truth, away from our connectedness with our soul, and away from spiritual growth. When an individual chooses to be herself and live her truth, she invariably chooses love.

A person can be herself without living her truth or choosing love, but she cannot be on the spiritual path unless she chooses love.

At any point in time, an individual's vibration exists at a specific frequency rate that provides an upper and lower limit to the range of compatible choices. Evolved individuals have accelerated vibrations and a wider range of possible choices. Unevolved individuals have slower vibrations and therefore make choices within narrower limits. When an individual's vibration falls and then moves outside of love's sanctity, unloving choices become compatible and acceptable. Choosing outside of love does not conflict with the basic self when the vibration of self is low. But being outside of love is also outside of the spiritual path. The evolved individual, on the other hand, is attuned with her truth and soul, has risen above the blockages and illusions created by physical density, and makes choices that reflect love. Evolved or unevolved, choices made are consistent with the limits of personal vibration. The unevolved individual has the opportunity to make loving choices that lead to spiritual growth, and the evolved individual knows enough to choose love always.

Our basic nature leads us to love and spiritual endeavour. If an individual is unevolved, choosing love and the spiritual path is usually overwhelmed by illusion and density. If evolved, love is the natural choice following the free-will to aspire towards the true self, i.e., a being of love. Although choices on Earth are free, the result is predictable according to the quality of an individual's love vibration. When love is abundant, our choices express love and make the spiritual path possible. Because only the choice of love brings about spiritual growth, having the freedom to choose outside of love is itself an illusion. For the spiritual person—as in heaven, so on Earth—the choice is one expression of love or another.

3.11 Love's Role in Empowerment

Love is the key to making our mission to fulfill God's will on Earth work. Love prepares the fetus before birth; love prepares the base chakra to receive spirit-light; love opens the base chakra; and love is the guiding light for enlightenment. Further, the love of the soul, expressed through the release of its seed-light from the base chakra, opens the upper chakras. In the same way as love prepares the base chakra to receive the light of the soul, love also prepares each of the upper chakras to receive the light of empowerment. Love makes the spiritual path possible.

Even before manifesting within the body, the upper chakras are encoded to open only to soul light, and therefore, to vibration that is very high and subtle. By opening and accepting the frequencies of the seed-light released from the base chakra, the vibration of each of the upper chakras rises. Raised vibration is better able to attract, anchor, and assimilate the frequencies needed to effect empowerment than is dense vibration. The faster the vibrational rate of any manifest form, the better it will work with light. Because love is the ultimate presence capable of raising vibration, adding love from the seed-light or from any other source, opens the way for the frequencies of empowerment to enter the chakras and be assimilated.

Once the upper chakras have been opened, each of them eventually makes its own contribution to the enlightenment process. The base chakra was the first to contribute; the heart chakra is the second. Before the heart can do its job, it too, must be opened by the soul's seed-light and empowered. Once empowered, the heart offers love. As love is so clearly integral to the spiritual path, the heart chakra's contribution is essential. Love from the heart chakra raises the vibration of the body's other chakras.

The procedure leading to empowerment follows the same sequence every time. First, the seed-light frequencies and then the empowerment light frequencies accumulate within, thus strengthening the presence of the Oneness. Because Oneness has the creative power of the God-self, it also has the power to create light. In the empowered heart, the light created is love.

Love from the heart enters the chakra distribution system and then enters each of the other chakras. As the love vibration from an individual's own heart is perfectly attuned with the body's overall frequency rate, there is no question about its compatibility. Heart chakra love is easily accepted in each of the other chakras.

Heart-love has its own importance. The heart chakra is the one source of love that allows a person to be completely independent. With love supplied from the heart within, the individual's vibration can be raised without the need for love from external sources. As a source for love, the contribution of the heart chakra is continuous throughout life.

Love accelerates any essence it touches. Love from the heart, from the seed-light of the base chakra, or from external sources, each accelerate the essence of the chakras. Chakra vibrations then rise and open to receive the frequencies of light that empower its essence. Without love, however, the essence of the chakras remains at a lower and denser vibration, blocking the entry of light needed for empowerment. Unempowered chakras cannot contribute to the enlightenment process. They cannot fulfill the tasks they were designed to carry out. Love is the essential ingredient that makes empowerment possible.

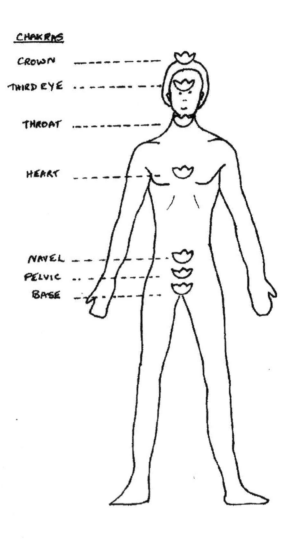

Chapter 4: Empowering the Incarnation

4.1 The Light of Empowerment

The opening of the base chakra and subsequent rise of the seed-light brings the presence of the soul out of dormancy. But the seed-light does not empower the bodily form with light. The light frequencies needed to empower the body, including the chakras, are different from the frequencies of the soul found in the seed-light. Soul frequencies are created exclusively by the soul and resonate throughout the body, but do not embody the spectrum of frequencies needed to effect its empowerment. Empowerment frequencies are specific only to the one part of the body for which they were intended and originate primarily from sources external to the self, including the higher dimensions, the Earth, or even other physical beings.

The empowerment of the body takes place one step at a time, with the assimilation of one frequency after another. Each frequency is created for one specific part of the body. The empowering frequencies intended for the navel chakra resonate only with the navel chakra and, more precisely, only with one specific light receptor within the navel chakra. Light for the throat chakra resonates only with the throat chakra, and so on. The navel chakra cannot assimilate frequencies intended to empower the throat chakra; and the frequencies themselves are incompatible with any manifest form for which they were not intended. More crucially, the order in which they are assimilated is strictly sequential with the lowest frequencies being assimilated before the higher frequencies. With each frequency that unites with its intended form, empowerment strengthens, Oneness expands, form evolves, and the process towards full enlightenment moves forward.

The chakras are the body's premier forms capable of assimilating

115

light. They are designed to work with light. Because of the chakra distribution system and matrices of light receptors, their vibrations are set up to attract and assimilate light in an organized orderly way. Each chakra plays its own important role in the enlightenment process.

What does an empowered chakra do? How do the individual chakras contribute to the enlightenment process?

4.2 Base Chakra: Environmental Compatibility

The base chakra has a role in accommodating the seed-light of the soul at birth, but is also the lowest of the chakras. It is the closest chakra to the Earth both literally and in its vibration. The base chakra directly incorporates the vibrations of the heavens through the seed-light and directly incorporates the vibrations of Earth through proximity. Being intimate with the soul is crucial in creating harmony between the individual and the heavens; and being intimate with the Earth is crucial to generating harmony between the individual and his physical surroundings. Because the base chakra works in both realms, it can serve as the bridge between heaven and Earth. The combination of heavenly and Earthly vibrations makes its position among the chakras quite unique and sets it apart to serve the enlightenment process in equally unique ways.

Some of the base chakra's important roles have already been mentioned. Its role in anchoring and protecting the soul's seed-light was explained with in chapter three. Its additional responsibility for setting the overall vibrational frequency rate within the individual, however, was only briefly mentioned (see section 3.5) and needs further clarification. Understanding the part played by the empowered base chakra in determining the physical body's overall vibrational rate will help with understanding its primary task, that of environmental compatibility.

The overall vibration rate determines how well the individual harmonizes with her immediate environment. The places to which a person goes in life, the vibrations she resonates with, and the environments that are conducive to growth are directly related to the individual's overall vibration. The base chakra's ability to incorporate and reflect the overall vibration helps position the individual where she can best achieve the assimilation of light.

Establishing the overall frequency rate within the incarnate individual is not the same as assimilating light or raising vibration. Establishing the rate refers to the harmonization of all frequencies contained in the body to yield a unified consistent vibration throughout the individual-as-a-whole. The unified vibration is not manipulated by the base chakra, but is brought together and centralized within the base chakra.

The vibration of an individual on Earth has its own unique frequency rate. Similarly, the vibration of the immediate environment in which the individual finds herself is also unique. As there are millions of individuals and millions of immediate environments on Earth, the number of different vibrational frequency rates is beyond any attempt to measure. Most important, the individual is best suited to the Earthly environment that has a similar vibrational rate to her own.

Like seeks like. The individual seeks the worldly circumstances into which she fits. The prima ballerina vibrates at a rate that is compatible with dancing for a professional ballet company. The trainee, who recently graduated from the hotel management course, fits best in an entry-level position, learning the hotel trade. For each individual, one specific environment suits best.

Being in a place that is compatible provides comfort. Any perceived lack of comfort indicates the differences between the vibration rate of the individual and the vibration rate of her immediate surroundings. Consider the discomfort of the resistance fighter sitting in a Nazi Gestapo prison during the second world war. The vibration rate of the resistance fighter and the vibration rate of the prison are very different and very incompatible. The light frequencies in the prison represent everything that the resistance fighter's base chakra is programmed to avoid. An individual thrives in compatible surroundings, but incompatible surroundings can truly be a challenge.

For an incarnate individual, the most compatible environment possesses the specific light frequencies needed for empowerment.

To be empowered as a real-estate salesperson, taking the sales training courses, participating in the activities of the community, and studying the market combine to place the individual in the environment necessary for success. Exposure to the light frequencies found in the real-estate environment leads to assimilation and subsequently to empowerment as a realtor.

To be empowered with confidence, the grade-four elementary school student studies her geography lessons and passes the exam. By building her knowledge base and working to pass, she places herself in position to receive frequencies that empower her with confidence.

To be empowered as a ballerina, the individual first goes to ballet school. By attending practice lessons, and by learning balance, coordination, concentration, and graceful movement, she exposes herself to the light found in the ballet-school environment. When she has assimilated the light frequencies she needs, she becomes empowered to be the ballerina she aspires to be.

The salesperson, the student, and the ballerina each thrive within the environment having the light frequencies needed for their empowerment.

Because the base chakra carries the vibration of the individual-as-a-whole, it has been given responsibility for attracting the environment most consistent with the individual and her path in life. It sets the agenda for the types of experiences encountered in daily life. The empowered base chakra either attracts the needed physical-level environment to the individual, or it creates the circumstances that move the individual to the place she is best suited. A person's role, friends, social position, and career are all consistent with her overall vibration, as reflected in the base chakra. The base chakra influences an individual's directions in life to ensure that the places the individual finds herself are compatible.

Once an individual has found her own compatible space, she continuously receives and assimilates light frequencies found within that space. An environment of satisfaction breeds satisfaction. An environment of confidence breeds confidence. An environment of success breeds success. With every frequency acquired, her vibration rises, her Oneness expands, and she evolves. Being in the right place and having the right light frequencies available provides the individual with the opportunity to grow into the enlightened state at an optimum rate.

The light frequencies available within any one venue of life are, however, finite. Eventually, the individual assimilates all the light she can and, therefore, accomplishes all the growth possible. If she remains in the same space without exposure to new light frequencies, her evolution will come to a halt, and her life path will stagnate. She will need to change venues to continue growing.

After an individual has assimilated all the light from a particular environment, the empowered base chakra creates the circumstances that push the individual toward the next environment. With each frequency assimilated, the individual's vibration rises to match and exceed the vibration of the immediate environment. During the process, the base chakra continuously integrates the body's overall vibration within itself. As the body becomes empowered and its Oneness expands, the base chakra simultaneously becomes empowered and its Oneness also expands. When no new frequencies are available, assimilation and expansion stop. A new environment becomes necessary for further growth. The expanded and empowered base chakra then strengthens its attraction for new light frequencies and initiates the shift from the current venue to a new one.

Whenever a person moves from one venue to another, a new and different set of light frequencies becomes available. A day job as a bank teller helps a person acquire the light frequencies of patience and tolerance for the public. The bank teller can also acquire the frequencies of spatial perspective, of appreciation for beauty, and of colour harmonization by taking oil-painting classes in the evening. A person can be exposed to several venues per day. The frequencies found in the workplace are different from the frequencies found in the lunchroom, and different again from the frequencies at the hairstylist shop. Each venue has different frequencies to offer. The base chakra is responsible for matching the individual with the most beneficial places-to-be.

If the individual remains in the same venue receiving the same light frequencies for a lengthy time period, the patterns of life ossify and growth is put on hold. Stagnation prevents the natural flow and expansion of light, but only to a point.

The base chakra continuously expands and grows by assimilating the light found in the external environment, but also expands and grows by assimilating light generated through the creative power of its own inner Oneness. Growth continues on the strength of the light frequencies created within, even after all the frequencies available from the local environment have been exhausted. The vibration of the base chakra, and thereby, the overall vibration of the individual, and the vibration of the local environment grow apart. Tension rises within the base chakra as environmental incompatibility increases. When the growing base chakra's vibration is strong enough, disruption occurs and the individual is liberated to find a new environment.

At times, breaking free of the old environment causes dramatic eruptions. A teenager needs more and fresh light frequencies to evolve. Because she lives under controlling parents, she rebels and runs away from home. She may not find a more suitable environment for growth immediately, but she will have broken free of the stagnation that was preventing her growth. In contrast, an individual, who is open-minded and free of constraints, has the flexibility to move easily from one life situation to another. Whether the energies causing the shift to a new venue flow smoothly or rise to eruption, the empowered base chakra eventually shifts the individual into the space needed for continued growth.

Romantic relationships provide another example to illustrate how situations in life can either lead to growth or cause stagnation. In the first instance, two lovers share each others' vibrations. Each lover comes with his or her own complement of light frequencies that then becomes available to the other lover for assimilation and growth. If the love they share is powerful enough, the channels to receive light stay open. Each individual in the relationship grows by virtue of the light attracted to their combined vibration, as well as the light created within each individual. The romantic relationship works well because each lover makes a contribution and benefits from the contribution of the other.

In contrast, the basis for some relationships is merely a life lesson the lovers share in common. During their time together, each lover offers and receives light frequencies to learn the lesson. Once the lesson has concluded, the flow of light between the two lovers ends and, so too, will the relationship. Each lover will need to move on to a different situation to acquire the light frequencies needed for continued growth.

The illustration of the romantic relationship has a further perspective. The vibration of one of the lovers may be growing faster than the vibration of the other. Or perhaps, the base chakra of one of the lovers is empowered, but the base chakra of the other lover is not. As the empowered lover's base chakra continues to strengthen its attraction for the light needed for growth, the vibrations of the two lovers grow apart. Separation takes place when the tension in the base chakra, arising from the need to seek new light frequencies, is greater than the bond holding them together.

The base chakra has another major role not already mentioned. The base chakra is the seat of the will of the individual on Earth. Because life is driven by the energies of spirit within an Earthly and grounded context, housing the will in the base chakra is ideal. The base chakra incorporates both soul and Earth vibrations and can extend those influences upon the will most readily. By design, with the help of the base chakra, the will is able to align directly with the soul's seed-light, as well as ground itself firmly within the Earth's vibration.

Survival is a further role ascribed to the base chakra in which the will is important. In the most crucial aspect of survival, i.e., the threat to life, the will to survive is primary. The will is intimately connected with the soul's seed-light and can, therefore, bring significant soul energies to bear. At the same time, because the base chakra is well attuned to the Earth's frequencies, the will can also draw upon the resources of the physical plane by working with the light of the planet. When an individual's survival is threatened, the will, centred within the base chakra, is most capable of marshalling both physical and soul energies for survival.

Survival inspires the perception of life-threatening situations, but survival also implies continuity. That is, an individual vibrates at a particular frequency rate, and if the individual continues to vibrate at the same rate, she survives. Survival, then, also refers to the continued maintenance of an individual's vibration at the current rate. Death and threats to well-being are not at issue. The ballerina is not concerned about death when she attends dance practice. But when she is recognized for her talent and is asked to join a dance company, she survives as a ballerina. She thrives! Similarly, the engineering student, who passes his second-year exams and moves into third year, survives as an engineering student. The principle of bringing the will and the energies, coordinated through the base chakra, to bear upon well-being is the same whether the need is to allay a threat to life or to maintain one's vibration.

The empowered base chakra ensures that an individual is in the right place at the right time to acquire the light she needs. Each change in venue provides a unique set of light frequencies that contribute to the further expansion of the individual's Oneness on Earth. Change, however, can also mean numerous abrupt and possibly radical shifts in location, occupation, relationships, life-styles, and perceptions. In each instance, traumatic or gentle, the empowered base chakra incorporates the overall vibrational rate of the individual and works to find the environment best suited for optimal survival on the path to enlightenment.

4.3 Pelvic Chakra: Attraction/Repulsion

Each of the body's seven major chakras was designed to take the processing of light a step further. The first and lowest of the chakras, the base chakra, works to ensure that the individual is placed where light is abundant. The second chakra, the pelvic chakra, facilitates the assimilation of light frequencies by amplifying the polarity of magnetic fields wherever they are found within the physical body.

To grow and evolve on Earth, manifest forms, including the human body, need to be exposed to light. If assimilated, some frequencies, contribute to empowerment, enlightenment, and the expansion of Oneness. Other frequencies either make no contribution or work to lower or even destabilize vibration. The evolution of the incarnate being follows the assimilation of one light frequency after another, whenever wanted frequencies are attracted and unwanted frequencies are repelled.

The second chakra contributes to the evolutionary process by strengthening the attraction for the light frequencies needed for growth and by strengthening the repulsion of frequencies not needed. It amplifies polarity differentials. Throughout the body, molecules, cells, groupings of cells, and even body organs emit a negative or positive polar charge that attracts or repels light frequencies for growth. The charge, weak or strong, can be strengthened by the addition of pelvic chakra energy. Pelvic chakra energy attaches to the charged magnetic fields within the body, increasing their strength and their ability to attract and repel.

Pelvic chakra energy is created within the pelvic chakra's own Oneness then radiates to every other part of the body, primarily through the channels of the chakra distribution system. When pelvic chakra energy encounters a charged magnetic field, it attaches itself to the field, enhancing its strength. Because both negative and positive energies radiate from the pelvic chakra separately, negative pelvic-chakra energy attaches to negatively charged fields within the body; and positive pelvic-chakra energy attaches to positively charged fields. The body's existing polarity differentials increase, and the ability of the empowered body part to attract frequencies for assimilation increases, along with its ability to repel unwanted frequencies.

The pelvic chakra makes a notable contribution to the base chakra's primary responsibility of placing an individual in the environment best suited for his growth. It contributes to the base chakra's effort to relocate the individual once the needed frequencies of the local environment have been exhausted.

The pelvic chakra supplies energy to each of the physical body's existing magnetic fields until the field is neutralized by the assimilation of light. If light is unavailable, however, the field's polarity continues to grow, as it receives more and more of the pelvic chakra's energies. Either the field attracts the necessary frequencies from its local environment, or its attraction strengthens even more. Eventually, the increase in polarity causes a shift in the body's overall vibration, along with an incongruence with the local environment. The change in the body's overall vibration is incorporated into the vibration of the base chakra, which then goes to work to place the individual into a new environment, which contains the fresh frequencies needed for continued growth.

The process of empowerment is a cycle, that starts with an individual's arrival in a place having an abundance of frequencies needed by that individual. Thereafter, assimilation of available light begins. By strengthening the polarity differential within, the pelvic chakra's energy strengthens the body's attraction for light. Available frequencies are assimilated by magnetic fields which then return to their neutral state. The pelvic chakra, however, continues to strengthen the body's remaining charged fields. Because the light needed to neutralize the charged fields is unavailable, the increasingly stronger charge reinforces the shift to a new location, and the cycle starts over again. With each repetition of the cycle, newly assimilated frequencies enhance empowerment.

Sex is associated with the pelvic chakra because it is related to the attraction function. Sex attracts one person to another, but attraction is also generated by projecting beauty, by acting in kindness, by being generous, and by being considerate. Each aspect of personality radiates its own set of light frequencies. Human individuals are walking storehouses for light and are important sources of light for other individuals. By enhancing polar differentials already existing within an individual's vibration, such as sexuality, generosity, and consideration, the pelvic chakra participates in the attraction of light and the attraction of other individuals having light.

Anger is also associated with the pelvic chakra. Anger relates to the repulsion function. It creates disharmony and separation. It is one of the most effective ways for one person to remove another person from his space. When the person is removed, so too are all that person's light frequencies. Insults, judgements, rudeness, and laying blame are equally effective. An angry individual generates a strong energy field that is further strengthened by pelvic chakra energies. The pelvic chakra simply supplies energy to the existing negatively charged polar fields to strengthen their ability to repel.

The attraction-repulsion functions of the pelvic chakra can be as overt as sexuality and anger, but are most often extremely subtle. At minute molecular levels, the body's form generates attraction for the frequencies it needs, but the attraction is usually very weak. Pelvic chakra energies attach themselves to any polarity field they encounter—negative or positive, weak or strong—and thereby amplify the field's strength. In summary, the pelvic chakra further empowers the body to attract wanted light frequencies and to repel unwanted frequencies found in the person's immediate environment. It thus contributes to the potential for assimilation, and thereby, to the enlightenment process.

4.4 Navel Chakra: Form Expansion

The navel chakra is the third chakra.

While the second chakra sorts out which frequencies are desirable, the third chakra expands the space into which light can enter to be assimilated.

The physical form assimilates light. Essentially, it is a space that vibrates at a frequency rate in harmony with desirable light frequencies. As more light assimilates, form's vibration rises allowing it to work with progressively more and higher frequencies. At some point, the vibration of the form reaches its optimum level in terms of both the quality and quantity of frequencies it can accommodate. Thereafter, it assimilates frequencies no higher than its own vibration and no more that its form can hold. Form's vibration has finite limitations. Because form is finite, progress upon the spiritual journey is also finite.

The first two chakras can place a person in the appropriate places to acquire light and set the body's polarity to enhance assimilation. They can even contribute to the relocation of the person to more light-rich venues. However, at some point, the amount of light that the physical body can hold reaches saturation. Regardless of the frequencies immediately available, the body cannot hold more light of any kind. In this situation, spiritual growth stops.

The problem of finite vibration, and therefore limited spiritual growth, is resolved by the creative potential of the navel chakra.

Throughout the universe, the power to create arises from the God-self found in the presence of the Oneness. Oneness wherever it exists, including the Oneness in the body, possesses the power to create. Once the navel chakra has been empowered by the assimilation of light into its form, it, too, becomes Oneness with the power to create.

The creative power of the navel chakra is used to increase the capacity of the bodily form to receive light. The navel chakra uses its creative power to create more form. The space within form, into which light is assimilated, expands. With more room for light, form surpasses its previous limits and assimilates more light. Form assimilates more, but also higher frequencies of light if they are available. The resumption of assimilation means a resumption in spiritual growth.

The most readily available source of higher light frequencies is near at hand. The process of assimilation is affected by the vibration of both form and light. Light, which crosses the threshold from higher dimensions into the third dimension, splits. The dense aspects of any one light frequency penetrate onto the physical plane. The high and subtle aspects remain in the heavens. Between the low and dense aspects and the high and subtle aspects, a third aspect of the same frequency positions itself in stasis between heaven and Earth. The third aspect remains suspended within the individual's etheric body. Because the third aspect vibrates too fast to fully descend onto the physical plane, but slowly enough to cross the threshold from the heavens, it is unable, but only marginally, to move onto the physical plane. Compared to the low and dense aspect, which readily resonates with physical form, the third aspect is slightly higher and more subtle. The third aspect is not immediately available to the Earth plane. But because it sits within the etherics, it is within reach.

The light that remains in the etherics is the most immediate source of higher light frequencies available for assimilation. Form that is expanded and elevated may vibrate fast enough to attract and assimilate the higher vibrations of the third aspect.

The capacity of an individual's vibration to assimilate light is relatively stable over time, but increases with the influence of the navel chakra. When the creative power of the navel chakra goes to work, it expands form wherever expansion is needed in the body. The navel chakra does not interfere with the light-anchoring capacity of any existing form. Rather, it creates more of the same form at a slightly higher vibration to complement that which already exists. The newly expanded and slightly higher form has the capacity to attract and assimilate higher and more subtle frequencies including the third aspect of frequencies sitting in stasis in the etheric body. Once the higher frequencies have a place to go to, they move out of stasis and onto the physical plane. By creating a subtle expansion of form, the navel chakra provides a compatible space into which higher frequencies can be assimilated.

Because the navel chakra creates only a marginal expansion of existing form, the difference it makes is hardly noticeable. Over time, however, the accumulated effect of each additional higher frequency assimilated profoundly contributes to the enlightenment process.

4.5 Heart Chakra: Love and Compassion

Love is the essence of light. All vibration pulses. Love helps the pulses go faster.

The magic of love is its ability to accelerate vibration. When vibration is fast enough, light enters, assimilates, and empowers. Love and compassion are the heart chakra's contributions to the enlightenment process.

Of the infinite numbers of light frequencies available in the universe, love pervades all, but specific frequencies belong to the love vibration. The heart chakra is the gateway through which the light of love frequencies is channelled from sources in the heavens. The empowered heart also uses its own Oneness to create its own love frequencies from within. Love is created in the heavens and in human hearts.

In the heavens, love is all encompassing. It surrounds and embraces all vibration without reserve. All within the heavens is light and Oneness and love simultaneously. Light frequencies meander gently in and out of any vibration that generates a mere whim of attraction. Light floats in the sea of love, ebbing and flowing with the tides of universal bliss. All form in the heavens is love, and is in perfect harmony with all light.

In contrast, on Earth, light moves towards physical form that vibrates fast enough to give it a home. Vibration is not surrounded by love; and separation is pervasive. Some physical forms vibrate fast enough to accept light, while other forms are slow and dense and full of blockages. On Earth, light can only go where it is welcome. Love contributes by opening physical form to accept and assimilate light. Love reconditions form by accelerating form's vibration. It makes form less dense and more compatible with higher and more subtle light frequencies. In the heavens, light moves anywhere at will through the omnipresent medium of love, but on Earth, light moves to and from mediums of form that have been enhanced by love.

Love's contribution to the flow of light can be understood by the influence it has on form. The model of the atom helps to illustrate. As electrons orbit the nucleus, they occupy the space of the atom. Slower electrons occupy space for a longer period, while faster electrons move in and out of space quickly. By moving at a faster frequency rate, the opportunity for light to move between the electrons increases. When form vibrates faster, it can accommodate a greater number and a wider range of frequencies. When love is the energy behind the movement of the atom's electrons, the electrons move faster. The greater the love, the faster the movement and the greater the amount of light that can move through form.

In addition to creating love, the heart chakra also creates compassion. Compassion is the calling card for love. To be touched by compassion is to be invited into the grace of the love centre.

Love, in the absence of compassion, is raw and blinding and only available to individuals, who can perceive the divinity of love's truth laid bare. The intensity of unmasked love on Earth is too great for most individuals. Those, who are not evolved, seek to protect themselves from love's overwhelming brilliance. But when love is accompanied by compassion, the journey to love becomes a gentle process accessible to anyone.

The light of compassion is constructed from a vortex of frequencies including kindness, joy, happiness, acceptance, respect, warmth, and gratitude, among many others. Each frequency within the vortex is like an open doorway with a smiling hostess beckoning interested individuals to step through. As the individual walks through compassion's many doorways, he steps into love's divine space. When he experiences a person's kindness, he opens to experience that person's love. When he experiences acceptance, he opens to love. The frequencies of compassion radiate outward to touch the hearts of loving beings, bringing them into the embrace of the love centre.

With love at the core, the vortex of compassion swirls all around. Although compassion usually surrounds the love centre, love is a complete and independent vibration. It can stand alone without compassion. Compassion, on the other hand, arises from love and cannot stand alone.

Compassion is only genuine when love is at the core. The Boy Scout, who extends kindness to help the elderly person across the road, acts with compassion from his heart of love. In contrast, if the used car salesperson extends warmth and appears to be generous for the purpose of convincing a customer to buy a car that needs repair, he is not acting out of love. Without love at the centre, compassion is like the donut—it surrounds nothing. True compassion extends from love. It radiates outward from love to surround love and to embrace any vibration coming into its sphere.

Each frequency in the vortex of compassion ushers compatible vibrations into the sanctuary of love. For example, a heart of love, with a vortex of peace swirling round, is a magnet for any individual who resonates with peace. Peace draws the individual into the vortex of compassion and, thereby, into love's embrace at the centre. As another example, a loving heart, surrounded by the vortex of warmth, attracts individuals who resonate with warmth. Each individual, who enters the embrace of warmth, is swept inward toward love at the centre. Compassion reaches out to bring us to love.

By aligning with the frequencies of compassion, an individual can enter the space of another individual freely. Compassion creates ease of interaction. Without compassion, however, our contemporaries are forced to knock at love's door, but are also forced to prepare themselves for the blinding flash when it suddenly opens. Compassion shines its light marking the pathway to love's door. It is the merge lane for traffic coming onto the highway of love. Who could resist the feelings of respect, peace, kindness, acceptance, generosity, contentment, warmth, happiness, joy, and more, as love uses the vortex of compassion to touch our hearts and bring us into its embrace?

On Earth, where love is found here and there within the void of physical space, compassion is like the flower petal that says, "Come smell my scent and see my beauty." Love cannot be taken for granted on Earth because it is not omnipotent. Frequencies of compassion are needed to provide the assurance that love can be found within. When individuals hear the sounds of a warm voice or sense the offering of generosity, they allow themselves to experience warmth and generosity, and then allow themselves to move into the love centre. Compassion works to remove the fears, doubts, and hesitations that cause resistance to the flow of vibration into love's space. Compassion makes way for a person to be open and vulnerable and to embrace the spirit of love.

Although compassion works on Earth to bring external vibrations into love's embrace in the same way as in the heavens, a basic difference exists. In the heavens, love is everywhere. Compassion extends from the love centre where it originates, through the omnipresent vibration of love, to any corner of the lighted universe. It journeys through the medium of love without limits. In the heavens, compassion is infinite. In stark contrast, on Earth, compassion extends only to the limits of its vortex. Beyond the vortex lies the density of physical vibration. Love and compassion project outward from the heart, but, once they extend beyond the boundaries of their origins, they dissipate into the blackness of physical density and become lost. Compassion in the heavens gently reaches outward to any distance to offer love's invitation, but on Earth, it has limits. It reaches only as far as it can into the density of the third dimension.

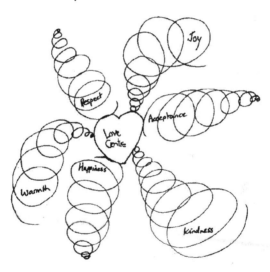

Vortices of Compassion

The heart chakra channels the frequencies of love and compassion, and creates them from within. Equally important, the heart works with light that passes through the chakra distribution system. Light continuously travels between and through each of the chakras along the distribution system's pathways. As a light frequency passes through the heart chakra, it is reconditioned by the love essence of the heart. Love accelerates the passing frequency, raises its vibration, and sends it on its way. The reconditioned frequency then carries the heart's love wherever it goes.

As compassion issues forth from the love in our hearts, other beings of light surrender to its attraction. Compassion delivers us into love's embrace. Love, then, goes to work to raise vibration to open form to light, and to empower.

4.6 Throat Chakra: Truth

Between the upper chakras and the heart is the fifth chakra, the throat chakra. The lower chakras: base, pelvic, and navel chakras, work directly with the vibrations of the physical plane and the physical body. The heart chakra accommodates light from both heaven and Earth. Above the heart chakra, the body works with progressively higher and more complex frequencies, as well as frequencies from above the physical plane. The throat chakra translates divine light into expressions of truth on Earth.

The throat chakra receives light through the crown chakra, but also from the third-eye chakra. The primary frequencies for empowerment step down from the higher planes through the crown and into the throat. Empowerment frequencies awaken and charge the throat chakra's form to perform its intended tasks, as they do for any other chakra.

The second source of light, the third-eye chakra, provides frequencies of consciousness. The throat chakra does not assimilate the incoming frequencies of consciousness, as it does for the frequencies of empowerment. Rather it uses consciousness frequencies to perform a processing function. It prepares light for expression on Earth as words, speech, and communication. Expression also takes on numerous other forms and is usually quite subtle. The throat chakra's ability to work with the light of consciousness reflects the increasing complexity of the upper chakras.

Because the throat chakra's job is the translation of light, understanding the throat chakra starts with understanding light. Light frequencies are created in the Godhead, as well as in an infinite number of creative centres throughout the lighted universe. Regardless of the creative source, each light frequency carries the divine frequencies of the Godhead at its core. As light travels outward from its source and through the heavens, it picks up frequencies additional to its core frequencies. By the time light finds its way onto the Earth plane, it is made up of both core frequencies from the Godhead, as well as auxiliary frequencies from numerous other creative centres in the heavens. The Earth itself and even the incarnate individual's host body create frequencies that can be added to the core.

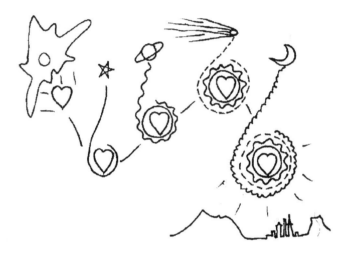

The core of a light frequency radiates from its origin, acquiring the influences of heavenly bodies, as it journeys to Earth.

The aggregate of core and auxiliary frequencies make up a complete light frequency with its own unique vibration and characteristics. It is made in the image of the creative sources from which it has arisen. The primary characteristic trait of the Godhead is divinity, and the primary characteristic trait of an auxiliary light source reflects that source. Light from the fifth-dimension reflects fifth dimensional characteristics. Light from the middle star of the Orion belt reflects the characteristics of the Orion belt. A light frequency carries the characteristics of both the divinity at its core and the auxiliary light sources that contribute to its uniqueness.

The throat chakra works with light frequencies and their imprinted characteristic traits to bring wisdom into expression.

The wisdom that comes with frequencies of light arrives in the language of light, but needs to be translated into the concepts and symbols of the third dimension before it can be used. The throat chakra can be compared to the computer chip. Information from myriads of data and assorted software programs passes through the chip and is processed from computer language into the words, numbers, or graphs that the human mind understands. Similarly, the throat chakra receives the light frequencies and the vibrational codes inherent to each frequency. After processing them, it creates expressions that manifest on the physical plane as symbols, words, gestures, and language that the incarnate mind can understand.

Each expression offered by the throat chakra reflects the characteristic traits of the light being processed along with the characteristic traits of the processor (throat chakra) itself. Among musical instruments, the sound made by blowing into a piccolo is vastly different than the sound of a trumpet. Similarly, the expression of truth emanating from the throat chakra of a corporate executive will be different than the expression emanating from the throat chakra of a student nurse. Each individual is a processor of light, different from any other. Even if two individuals are working with the very same light frequency, truth will be expressed differently for each.

To begin the processing of light, frequencies of consciousness are drawn into our incarnate form through the third eye. The third eye converts the light received into frameworks of symbols, that are understandable to our limited third-dimensional mind. The third eye edits or re-works frequencies of consciousness into packets of information, scrolls of wisdom, and bundles of usable physical energy. In turn, the throat chakra receives the processed frequencies and further translates them into words, oral speech, paintings, television programs, office memos, and advertising pamphlets. Less apparent expressions projected by the throat chakra also include a person's career path, preferred hobbies, choice of automobiles, and taste in clothes. The throat converts the language of the light into everyday expressions of who and what we are. It expresses the divinity within, our personal truth, externally.

The throat translates the frequencies available as it can. The quality of the light received, the ability of the individual to work with some, but not other frequencies, the density of the individual's processing mechanisms in the throat chakra, personal perceptions and opinions, and the immediate Earthly circumstances that make expression acceptable or unacceptable each contribute to the uniqueness of an individual's truth as brought forth to the outer world. Are we piccolo players or trumpet players? Are we long-winded or short-of-breath? Is the sound we make sweet or loud? The expression each of us projects is unique without question, even though the truth behind the expression is common to all. Truth is forever, but the expressions of it change with every moment.

Expressions emanating from the throat chakra are received by other individuals in terms that are often quite specialized. Wisdom to the university professor comes in information packets quite different from the information packets acceptable to the motor mechanic, but the process works in the same way. The language used in the university professor's dissertation on the philosophy of Plato's "Allegory of the Cave"[1], for example, will be vastly different than the language

1 Plato's "Allegory of the Cave" depicts a group of individuals who are chained inside a cave. They can look only in one direction—at the cave wall. Behind them is a fire, but they can see only the light that is casting shadows on the wall, not its source. Over time, the group has become attached to their own interpretation of the shadows. When one of their number is removed from the cave into the bright sunlight of the world outside, the interpretation of the shadows becomes instantly clear for the illusion it is. Upon the enlightened one's return, the interpretation of the world "beyond" is unacceptable to the limited vision of the group. He is cast out, persecuted, called a heretic

used in the manual for fixing fuel-injection gasoline engines.

When the throat chakra is called upon to express a specific packet of information in the external world, it translates the information into the patterns of language and conceptual thinking specific to the expressing individual. The professor uses the words, symbols, and dialectic of philosophy; the mechanic uses technical language. The light frequencies that make up the packet of information related to Plato's allegory are then transformed in the throat chakra into the professor's language and expressed in philosophical terms. Similarly, the frequencies used to understand the gasoline engine are converted into technical language and presented to the external world. Information, expressed through the throat chakra, enters the external world as specialized expressions of truth according to the medium (i.e., professor, mechanic) through which it is expressed.

After converting the language of light into the symbols and terms of the third dimension, the throat chakra projects an expression of the divine light frequencies of consciousness into the physical outer world. The language, springing forth from light, is the reflection of all of the characteristics of vibration and wisdom picked up during the light frequency's journey through the heavens as contributed by each of the auxiliary frequencies from each contributing source of creation, along with the wisdom of the core frequency as contributed by the creative source of the Godhead itself. On Earth, the outcomes are likely to appear ordinary—consoling a friend, arranging a meeting, conducting a phone conversation, and telling a joke. Divinity is expressed in terms that are perfectly attuned with the characteristics of the vibrations of light that pass through the throat chakra.

The throat chakra translates divine light into expressions of truth.

---

and ridiculed. In the new age, it is comforting to know that there are adequate numbers of individuals who have been exposed to the world "beyond". Rather, than suffering persecution, we will be leading the journey into the greater light.

4.7 Third Eye: Portal of Consciousness

The third-eye chakra is the portal through which the light frequencies of consciousness pass as they move between the soul in the heavens and the individual on Earth. It participates in the process of stepping up the vibration of frequencies on their way to the heavens and stepping down frequencies coming into consciousness.

The third eye is well located at the centre of the consciousness in the brain between the two physical eyes. From this vantage point, the frequencies of consciousness, sent from the soul to the third eye, move into the conscious mind relatively easily. Conversely, what a person sees on Earth is readily transmitted to the soul. By reading the light coming from the individual on Earth, the soul is informed of the individual's vibration and the vibrations of his immediate environment. The soul uses this information to determine, which frequencies and how much light it needs to send to the individual, to support his Earthly experiences. As the portal between the soul in the heavens and the incarnate mind on Earth, the third eye provides direct access in both directions.

When higher dimensional light frequencies of consciousness descend to Earth to enter the third eye, the process of conscious thought begins. Light, however, comes to the third eye in the raw forms of higher dimensional vibration and does not fit into the context of the physical plane. Its vibration is well above the range of frequencies available to human awareness. Processing, within the third eye, steps light down to a vibrational level usable within the physical context.

How is the Earthly human mind to recognize the meaning of light vibrations not based in the third dimension? The frames of reference, that bring understanding to thought, use the visions, symbols, and language of the Earth, not the heavens. The Earthly mind synthesizes thought from frequencies that carry meaning on the physical plane. The mind does not serve as the translator of heavenly consciousness into Earthly consciousness. Instead, the task of converting the frequencies of consciousness arriving from the heavens, into usable forms on Earth, belongs to the third eye.

The mind takes the light frequencies of consciousness, made usable in the third eye, and processes them further. Its intuitive side receives usable frequencies and refines them into the visions, symbols, and discernible language that can be understood by the intellect. These refined light frequencies become the building-blocks for thought that is recognizable within the context of Earthly experience.

To illustrate, the scientist ponders a problem within the complexities of the biochemistry of the living cell. His mind then attracts the higher vibrational frequencies of consciousness needed to complete his contemplation. The third eye takes the frequencies received and converts them into a usable format for the physical plane. It steps their vibrations down from higher-dimensional, outer-world frequency rates to a slower discernible Earthly frequency rate. The mind then uses the re-worked frequencies of consciousness to create thought within the Earth's own frames of reference. As more and more of the light of consciousness finds its way into the scientist's awareness, the solution to his initial problem becomes apparent.

Frequencies of consciousness originate in the heavens, but also originate on the physical plane. The third eye receives signals from the surrounding world after the eyes see and the ears hear. The traffic light turns green; the driver steps on the gas. In a split second, the driver's mind converts the stimulus of the green light into conscious action. Because the mind is directly connected to the third eye, the conscious experience on Earth can be viewed by the soul. Light frequencies are stepped up or accelerated in the third eye so they can be understood by the soul thus making physical experience available to the heavens.

The Earthly experiences, that rise up to become available to the soul, along with the wisdom that descends to become available to the mind, both depend upon the portal of the third eye and the light of consciousness. If the portal is only partially open, only a portion of the light can get through. Further, the frequencies that are stepped up or stepped down are the very delicate and often easily distorted frequencies of consciousness. If they are damaged, thought becomes damaged. If the contemplations of the mind are created from faulty components, the concepts and awareness that arise will also be faulty. The problem of a partially closed third eye and the further problem of poor quality light have the potential to seriously retard and distort human perceptions.

Because the third eye is the portal between the soul and the incarnate consciousness, the quality of the incarnate vibration affects the quality of the soul's connection, and thereby, the quality of the flow of light.

Incarnate vibration is crucial. The connection between the soul and the incarnate consciousness is possible only when the incarnate vibration approximates the vibration of the soul. The incarnate form must vibrate high enough to accommodate the higher and more subtle frequencies of the soul. Meditation, attending holy mass, prayer, and living love and compassion each contribute to raising vibration. The serious devotee, who acquires a spiritual discipline, sheds negative and attracts positive light frequencies for the purpose of raising vibration. When vibration is high enough, the soul connects, and soul light flows easily.

Raising vibrations through conscious efforts such as prayer are expressions of will and desire. Prayer, meditation, and the practice of compassion raise vibration as a matter of course. If these practices are done with conscious intent, the effect is significantly greater. Intent, expressed through will and desire, clarifies free choice. It brings the full strength of a person's energies to bear. It enhances the attraction of light into Earthly consciousness, and it strengthens the person's ability to radiate light to the heavens. When the flow of light in both directions is strong, the use of the portal of the third eye reaches its optimum.

The wilful effort to raise vibration through conscious intent is easily reversed whenever the mind is overcome by negativity. In the face of lower negative vibration, the flow of light through the third eye slows down or even stops. If the mind becomes enveloped in doubt, fear, hesitation, or any other negative thought-form, energy, that would otherwise be used to attract light to Earth or to radiate light to the heavens, is consumed by the effort to hold the negativity in place. The decrease in the flow of light through the third eye is proportional to the amount of energy needed to maintain the negative thought-form. Energy used for negativity cannot be used to attract or radiate light.

Negative energy works to retard the efforts of the third eye in other ways as well. For one, the soul's vibration is quite high and subtle. When negativity causes the overall vibration of the individual and the vibration of the third eye in particular to drop, the connection with the soul diminishes. The vibrations of the soul and the individual grow apart, eventually severing the link between the two. For another, the greater density of the third eye prevents it from working with higher and more subtle frequencies. In effect, the third eye closes to the higher frequencies needed for enlightenment. Negative energy lowers the capacity of the mind and of the third eye to process light. Their structural forms become dense and lifeless; they cannot do the tasks for which they were intended. Negativity has no positive effect upon the third eye or anything else.

To illustrate, contrast the effects of an attitude of cheerful optimism in your own workplace with an attitude of cynicism toward the company and its staff. Which attitude serves to attract the spiritual energy needed for a thriving environment that leads to growth? A good attitude works with higher and more subtle light; a bad attitude does not. A good attitude generates a higher overall vibration closer to the soul; a bad attitude does not. A good attitude opens the mind to receive the light frequencies of opportunity; a bad attitude does not. A good attitude contributes to a healthy happy environment because it attracts vibration and light that is healthy and happy; a bad attitude does not. With whom would you prefer to work?

The portal of the third eye opens to allow light to flow to and from the heavens thus providing consciousness for both the soul and the Earthly incarnation. When the third eye is fully open and aligned with the soul, the most subtle of frequencies move directly into the mind to surface as awareness. To be aware of the light frequencies that resonate with the third eye is to know the will of the heavens and truth on Earth. When the third eye is developed and empowered with vision, the mysteries of the light of consciousness are revealed.

4.8 Crown Chakra: Thousand Petal Lotus

The crown chakra is located at the top of the head in the most practical place from which to receive light from external sources. Its role is to receive and distribute light.

The crown chakra's millions of light receptors are arranged hierarchically. First, the crown's matrix of receptors create a singular attracting force. Individual receptors align their magnetic polarity fields with each of the other receptors to make the crown chakra into one big magnet for light. Next, subordinate to the crown chakra's unified magnetic field are sub-groupings of light receptors, that are organized into regional sub-fields and further organized into local sub-fields, each attracting specific ranges of frequencies. Finally, the individual receptor, standing alone, attracts the one light frequency specific to its vibration. In effect, the crown chakra is a maze of light receptors, each attracting its unique frequency, each contributing to the attraction of sub-ranges of frequencies, and each taking part in the overall attraction of light into the crown chakra.

The light attracted by the crown chakra is limited to frequencies that are able to pass through the etheric body. The etheric body filters light through its own magnetic attraction and repulsion, according to the needs of the individual's current vibrational state. But not all light is suitable. Therefore, not all of the available light attracted by the crown is capable of by-passing the scrutiny of the etherics. Some frequencies are drawn into the etheric body, while others are rejected. Although light frequencies entering the crown chakra are in harmony with the etherics, and thereby, with the individual, the quantity and quality of light is determined by the etheric field.

The light flowing past the etherics, into the crown chakra, is not distinguished by either its frequencies, nor its polarity.

First, the frequencies of incoming light are massed into one large stream. Once inside the crown chakra, however, the stream of light is broken down into increasingly more defined bands of frequencies. The crown is a graduated step-down series of receptor groups into which light flows. As the receptor groups become smaller and less generalized, the band of frequencies attracted narrows and becomes much more specific. Receptor groupings differentiate one band of frequencies from another. Each band is routed to the particular group of receptors, with which it resonates. The breakdown continues until the individual frequency is made available to its specific light receptor.

Second, the polarity of the crown chakra pulses in cycles from negative or yin polarity to positive or yang polarity. Half of the time, the crown attracts yin-charged frequencies; and the other of half the time, it attracts yang-charged frequencies. The crown chakra attracts the light frequencies that are specific to each of its receptors en masse and does so for both polarities.

The crown chakra's matrix of light receptors is neither fixed nor finite. At any one moment, the light coming into the crown is limited by the capacity of its millions of receptors to receive. The lower vibrational receptors are the first to open. As more of the light received is assimilated, more receptors open and the crown unfolds. With more opened receptors and more light to empower the crown chakra's form, its Oneness expands. The crown chakra's Oneness, as any Oneness, has the power to create. It creates more receptors to add to the crown's matrix. The number of receptors, therefore, is never static.

The crown chakra's matrix of receptors grows from within. It is the flowering thousand-petal lotus.

The crown chakra is capable of working with all ranges and frequencies of light. Light, having passed into the crown through the etherics, has already descended to Earth, and is therefore compatible with third-dimensional vibration. But beyond Earth, all light is of a higher dimension. The crown's receptors work with light that resonates on the third dimension, but they also work with light from the higher dimensions.

How so?

First, light is not limited to a single dimension. Light from the heavens or light on the third dimension is living light. The presence of God exists at its core. Regardless of the dimensional level at which a light frequency was created, the frequency can manifest on all dimensional levels simultaneously. A light frequency created on the sixth dimension, manifests in the fifth dimension through the realization of its inherent fifth-dimensional potential[2]. The same frequency manifests on the third dimension, through the realization of its third-dimensional potential, and manifests on the tenth dimension, through the realization of its tenth dimension potential. Light is multi-dimensional.

Second, light receptors are also multi-dimensional. They can access whichever dimension is most accommodating to bring a particular frequency to Earth. Receptors have a presence on the physical plane, as well as a presence in every higher plane, and are capable of interfacing with light in any dimension.

A receptor can reach up to the eighth dimension, for example, to connect with the frequency for which it was encoded. Although not limited by dimensional constraints, a receptor resonates with the one frequency, for which it was originally encoded. It does not resonate with any other. The receptor, once connected to its own

2 Language on our third dimension attempts to define the existence of life and vibration in higher dimensions. We may use the terms fifth, sixth, or twentieth dimension to illustrate our ideas. The fifth, sixth, or twentieth dimensions, however, are third dimensional concepts. What can we on the third dimension truthfully say about dimensions that do not conform to frames of reference that are limited to width, height, and depth, and the here and now? Is there a fifth dimension? Discussions of anyone on Earth can at best speculate about the qualities of higher dimensional existence. Suffice it to say that we need to communicate with each other in the symbols, ideas, concepts, and conventions upon which we can all agree. While reference is made to numbered dimensions, such as the fifth dimension, it is done knowing that a concept on the third dimension will always fall short of the truth of the concept in a higher dimension. The concept itself is a truth as far as the third dimension will allow.

frequency, brings the frequency's potential, as it exists in the eighth dimension, into realization in the third dimension. Therefore, frequencies, needed to satisfy the physical body's attraction for light, need not have a presence on Earth. Instead, the crown's receptors transcend the Earth plane into the higher dimensions where the frequency needed already exists. The crown's ability to attract light is therefore unlimited.

An incarnate individual's use of the multi-dimensional capability of her light receptors is determined by the quality of her personal Earthly vibration. For the person who is only marginally evolved and whose vibration is relatively basic, the crown chakra's receptors and matrix are limited to the third dimension and third-dimensional light. Before the receptors can interface with higher dimensions, the individual's vibration must rise. The receptors must vibrate fast enough to transcend the Earth plane and to resonate with the higher dimensions. Receptors operate multi-dimensionally, and the light received is limitless. For as much as an individual is evolved and her vibration is developed, her crown chakra's receptors can reach into higher dimensions. A person's ability to work with higher dimensional light frequencies is as good as her vibration.

The crown chakra fulfils its other primary role, the distribution of light, in two ways.

First, the crown chakra receives a broad range of light frequencies that resonate in various parts of the physical body. It is responsible for transferring light from its receptors to the chakra-distribution system and thereafter to the chakras. It also transfers light to the general bodily forms as best it can.

The light, attracted into the crown chakra, is distributed to the body through a number of light-conducting channel ways between the crown and places in the body. Although the majority of channel ways belong to the chakra distribution system, some, running primarily along the body's meridian lines, move light into the generalized body form, outside the chakras. Channel ways leading to the individual chakras are highly specialized, but in most parts of the body, channel ways are either quite primitive or non-existent.

Light frequencies are distributed from the crown chakra through polar attraction and repulsion. Light receptors in the crown chakra carry a polar charge to attract light. When a light frequency, carrying the opposite polar charge, enters a receptor, the receptor's charge is neutralized and brought into balance. The frequency then moves from the receptor into the first of a series of sub-units that comprise the conducting distribution channel way. At rest, the sub-unit of the channel way carries a neutral charge. When the polar charge of the crown chakra's receptor shifts to neutral because of the presence of a light frequency, the channel way sub-unit closest to the receptor becomes charged. The sub-unit's polarity then attracts the light frequency out of the receptor into itself. The receptor returns to its usual charged polar state, and the first sub-unit becomes neutral in the presence of the light frequency. The second sub-unit of the channel way undergoes the same shifts in its polar charge as the first sub-unit, and in turn, attracts the light frequency into itself. The light frequency moves from the receptor in the crown chakra, to the first sub-unit in the channel way, and to each successive sub-unit until it arrives at the light receptor for which it was intended. Thereafter, the frequency is assimilated to empower the body's form.

Second, the crown chakra distributes light to the incarnate being's subtle bodies including the emotional body, consciousness body, and Light Body.[3] The subtle bodies are not specific to any particular part of the physical body, but are pervasive throughout. They continuously surround and interact with every part of the physical

---

3 Depending upon which literary source reference is made, the subtle bodies generally include the etheric body, the emotional body, the consciousness body, and the Light Body. Typically, they are not physical; they are present as part of the incarnate form, and they interact in some way with the physical body. The Light Body, as distinguished from each of the other subtle bodies, is not present at birth. It will not be present at death either, unless the individual achieves adequate spiritual growth sufficient for the Light Body's invocation. Chapter Five presents a comprehensive discussion of the Light Body. The emotional body and consciousness body each warrant their own chapters in Volume Two of *The Story of Light*.

body including the crown chakra. Although the crown chakra attracts light intended for the subtle bodies, channel ways for distribution are unnecessary. Light moves from the crown to each of the subtle bodies directly.

The subtle bodies perform highly specialized tasks requiring highly specialized light frequencies. As a result, the crown chakra possesses a number of sub-groupings of light receptors specifically designed to direct light toward the intended subtle bodies. These sub-groupings do not facilitate the flow of any other light frequencies. Each of the light-receptor sub-groups connects directly to its particular subtle body, ensuring that light received in the crown chakra is transferred to the subtle body immediately.

The role of the crown chakra differs with each subtle body. Its role with the emotional body is perhaps the least complex. Light, intended for the emotional body's empowerment, is attracted into the crown, then transferred to the emotional body. The crown chakra also attracts and transfers light frequencies to empower the conscious body. Its further role, regarding the conscious body, is to provide the light frequencies specific to consciousness, needed to synthesize thought.

The crown chakra's role with the Light Body is more complex. The Light Body remains aloof from the physical plane and physical body until it has been invoked. The crown chakra's initial role is to facilitate the invocation process. When the time is right, the Light Body projects itself from its place in the heavens into the physical body through the crown chakra's specialized light-receptor sub-group, designed for this purpose. Once the Light Body is in place, the crown chakra continues to facilitate the movement of light from the higher planes into the Light Body on Earth.

The attraction of light from external sources is not exclusive to the crown chakra. The chakras, bodily form, and subtle bodies are all capable of attracting light on their own, but are not specialized for their role in attracting light. The crown chakra is specialized. The strength of the crown chakra's attracting force far surpasses the potential for attraction found anywhere else in the body.

146

4.9 Refraction and Distribution

To empower the chakras, a steady stream of light must flow through the chakra-distribution system and the chakras' matrices. Light normally flows easily. But if the flow is erratic, if light is subjected to too much third-dimensional density, or if the chakras are misaligned, empowerment takes longer.

In the process of light distribution, specific frequencies are selected for assimilation from the stream of light flowing through each chakra. Each chakra has its own matrix of light receptors, and each matrix is encoded to refract a unique range of light frequencies. Light flows into a chakra's matrix of light receptors, then proceeds to the next chakra, leaving behind the frequencies that were refracted. Differences in the structural configuration of each chakra matrix determines which frequencies are refracted and thereafter assimilated.

The development of the chakra-distribution system differs from the development of the chakras. Both the chakras and the chakra-distribution system open when the soul's seed-light rises from the base chakra. Both are reconditioned by the seed-light to work with their respective light frequencies of empowerment. The chakras are reconditioned to assimilate light, but the distribution system is reconditioned to conduct light. Further, the distribution system is reconditioned to protect light.

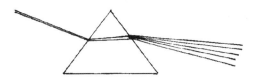

Refraction

The chakra-distribution system is set up through its system of polar charges and discharges to conduct light frequencies along its channel ways, but the same system of charges and discharges has a protection function as well. To begin, when the chakra-distribution system is in its neutral mode waiting to conduct light frequencies, its lack of charge neither attracts nor repels energies foreign to the individual's vibration. The channel ways do not normally need to expend energy to rid themselves of polluting energies and frequencies because foreign, and especially unwanted energies, do not accumulate in or around the channel ways. Without a polar charge, attraction is absent, therefore foreign frequencies have no place.

On the other hand, when light frequencies flow through the chakra-distribution system, polar charges result. Polar charges work to protect the flow of light. If an acceptable, positively charged light frequency enters the channel ways of the distribution system, the channel way assumes a negative charge to attract the frequency and keep it moving. The opposite is true for a negatively charged frequency. As both negatively and positively charged frequencies flow through the channel ways, the polarity of the channel way shifts continuously.

The polar charges, that rise and fall within the channel ways of the distribution system, leave no place for unwanted frequencies. When the channel way is positively charged, it actively attracts only frequencies that are intended for assimilation with specific receptors, and offers no means for other frequencies to find their way into its form. When negatively charged, the channel way actively repels all frequencies not intended for assimilation. Unwanted frequencies remain uninvited and are repelled from the chakra-distribution system's network of channel ways through the changes in polarity from positive to negative and from negative to positive that naturally occur whenever light frequencies move through its form.

Although protected, light moving through the chakra-distribution system is not without problems. First, light flowing through a chakra does not always resonate with the chakra's form. Only a single and specific light frequency, from among the thousands that pass through, will be attracted by a particular chakra light receptor. The individual receptor generates an insignificant magnetic force. Its weak attraction is not enough to help its light frequency find its way. But the problem is solved by creating light flow. When a frequency joins with many thousands of other frequencies, it is swept along in the flow. The manipulation of light into a flowing mass allows frequencies, that otherwise remain stationary, to move. Once on the move, they pass throughout the chakras and the body until they arrive at the receptor for which they were originally encoded. With close proximity, assimilation follows.

Second, within the chakra-distribution system, each chakra aligns with each of the other chakras, allowing the light to flow easily from chakra-to-chakra. When the chakras are aligned, a portion of the light passing through is readily refracted out and then assimilated by the appropriate chakra receptors. The remainder of the much larger flowing mass continues on to flow through the next chakra. If the chakras are not properly aligned, however, light is refracted in a haphazard fashion and can easily become lost or diverted to parts of the body for which it was not intended. A further portion of the light, that would otherwise flow into the next chakra, may flow out of the chakra-distribution system instead. Imbalances in the body and its chakras create misalignments, leading to the loss of light needed to effect empowerment.

Proper chakra alignment preserves the integrity of the flow of light as it passes through each chakra ensuring that each frequency arrives at the next chakra intact. As more and more frequencies pass through each chakra intact and in alignment, the opportunity for assimilation and subsequent empowerment is greater.

4.10 General Bodily Form

The enlightenment of the human physical body encompasses the entire body, not merely the chakras. Outside of the chakras, of the distribution channel ways, and of the subtle bodies, the human body consists of general bodily form. Therefore, every body part and every molecule has the potential to anchor and assimilate light.

The many channel ways of the chakra distribution system permit the ease of light flow, but do not extend into general body form. Although general body form is comprised of the same basic structure as the form found in the chakras, its design is not as complex as the chakras. It is not connected to the channel ways of the chakra-distribution system, and it has no specialized light receptors and no light receptor matrices.

General body form's attraction for light is dependent upon the individual receptor. In the chakras, and in the crown chakra in particular, individual receptors group together into matrices that generate strong magnetic attraction. In contrast, receptors of the general bodily form remain independent. Attraction arises from the strength of individual receptors acting alone and extends only as far as the receptor's own energy field. Compared to the size of an energy field emanating from a receptor matrix, the field of a single receptor is quite small. To be attracted by a receptor acting alone, a light frequency must be in very close proximity.

Within the general bodily form, light does not flow. Rather, it bounces from one light receptor unit to the next in haphazard fashion, comparable to a pinball bouncing from bumper to bumper or to a ping-pong ball in a box. A light frequency is either attracted or repelled by the polarity of the nearest receptor unit.

The empowerment process of generalized bodily form is considerably slower than that of the chakras. Light is pushed and pulled in every different direction, and its route is indirect and considerably longer. It navigates from one part of the body to another, but does so after changing course hundreds of times. Because general body receptors have a limited strength of attraction, each frequency will need to bounce randomly from receptor to receptor until it can come close enough to be attracted to the one receptor for which it was intended. In the absence of light flow, the individual light frequency takes much more time and effort to get into position for assimilation.

The absence of the flow of light within the body's form has implications for what needs to be done to improve the enlightenment process. When the receptors are arranged in a random pattern, the magnetic polarity they carry points in every direction. Negatively charged receptors oppose positive receptors, and vice versa. A great deal of a receptor's energy for attraction is lost when it is located near other receptors having opposing polarities.

How might the problem of opposing polarities be resolved?

If all the receptors in the general body form faced the same direction, light frequencies would flow, thus enhancing the body's exposure to light. When a person concentrates her thoughts on an idea or concept, her mind acts as a singular unit. It sets up a common polar charge involving a large number of light receptors all attracting light in the same way. Each receptor is energized by the mind's focus. By using the mind's energy to bring the body's receptors into alignment, light frequencies are attracted by a polar charge that is stronger and coordinated. Light flows. Frequencies move in harmony with other frequencies instead of opposing and bouncing off each other. As a result, the amount of light coming into the body's parts is substantially more, thus leading to much greater empowerment.

The ballerina, who is totally committed to her discipline, possesses focus. Every molecule and atom of her being is drawn into the harmony of her dance. Each body part joins with each other body part until their union leaves no separation. The energies that flow through the ballerina's body are linked to her singular purpose. The flow of energy that gives spirit to the dance is also the flow of light.

Mindful focus enhances the assimilation of light through the general body form, but so too does meditation. Meditation, free of any specific focus, creates serenity within the mind and consciousness. It eliminates the random jumble of uncoordinated thought-form energy and opens the consciousness to the larger universe, enabling connectedness with the soul.

Meditation does not create a flow of light frequencies as does the mind. Rather, meditation creates the serenity and calm needed to free the individual receptors to move within their own immediate spaces. As the serenity of meditation deepens, the polarity of the unimpeded individual receptor causes it to shift into harmonious alignment with its surrounding receptors. The attracting force of the individual receptor, although comparatively weak, is much more effective in an environment of calm. The devotee who meditates, seeking the serenity within, creates the harmony that allows light frequencies to be attracted deeply inside her body.

Similar to the chakras, general bodily form has been endowed with special and unique purposes.

The first special purpose involves the lower dimensions. Vibration exists within the dimensions above the third dimension, but it also exists below the third dimension. Light from the higher realms descends through successively lower dimensions before it arrives on Earth. And in turn, light descends through Earth's third dimension on its way to the dimensions below the third. Generalized bodily form creates space within itself, where the frequencies needed for communion with the lowest dimensions, can be given sanctuary. In effect, generalized form acts like a holding tank. The lower dimensional frequencies are drawn from the heavens into general body form and then transferred to both the lowest levels of the third dimension, as well as to the dimensions below.

In such low levels of vibration, consciousness is impossible; awareness is impossible. Nonetheless, light descends into form. Even below the level of the third dimension, light plus form results in the creation of Oneness, and thereby, the presence of God. The doorway, through which the I AM presence of the Godhead steps into the dimensions below the physical plane, is held open because of the general bodily form.

The second special purpose involves the general bodily form's crucial role in the biosynthesis of energy needed in the assimilation of light into form. Assimilation takes energy. The energy involved must be capable of working with both the body's physical vibration and the light frequencies to be assimilated.

In the human body, the energy needed to process the interaction of light with form comes from general bodily form. All of the chemical reactions occurring within the individual cells of general body form release light energy, which can be used for assimilation. When breath is drawn in and expelled, the chemical reactions that take place use and release the energy needed for the assimilation of light. The action and reaction of energies during digestion similarly use and release energy used for assimilation. General body form thereby provides energy through its normal bodily functions.

The energy directed to the assimilation of light is applied in two different ways. First, light energy is used to strengthen the polar charge of the light receptors: a greater charge means a greater attraction. And second, light energy is used to accelerate form's vibratory rate: faster vibration is better able to accommodate light. More light energy means stronger attraction and faster vibration, and thereby more assimilation.

Not all the energy intended for assimilation is used. Some energy enhances polar attraction and some accelerates form's vibration. The unused portion, the surplus, tends to be used more to accelerate form's vibration than to enhance polarity. Accelerating vibration is the preferred means to consume the surplus. Enhancing the polar charge enhances both positive and negative forms to receive energy. Whenever form is charged in one polarity but not the other, imbalance occurs. Using the surplus light energy to further empower polar charge leads to unwanted imbalance. On the other hand, when surplus energy is used to accelerate form, polarity is unaffected. To avoid polarity imbalances, surplus energy is used to accelerate form and not to enhance polar charges. An individual, suffering from enhanced polar charge, is sometimes labelled "hyper".

General body form is found in every part of the body outside the chakra system and the subtle bodies. Its specialized roles are to synthesize energy for light assimilation and to facilitate the movement of light into the lower dimensions. Light does not flow through general body form as it does through the channel ways of the chakra-distribution system. Rather, the harmony that facilitates the flow of light between individual body receptors comes with mental focus and meditation. Although generating harmony results in some amount of light flow, the empowerment of general body form is slow compared to the chakras.

Chapter 5: Enlightenment

5.1 Perspective

When Earth's foremost light-workers first arrived at the very beginning of time, they thought the Light Body would enter physical presence as a matter of course. The Light Body had been invoked into form in all the dimensions above the third dimension with few problems, so why should Earth be any different?

Earth was different.

The problem of third-dimensional density had not been anticipated. The physical body's vibration was much too slow to accommodate the Light Body or even to work with the light. More discouraging, the body could not be designed to work with light until its design had first dealt with the problems of physical survival. This meant that the job of invoking the Light Body into the physical body on Earth had to be held in abeyance for a considerable period of time.

Once the Earth's light-workers were able to enlighten the chakras, efforts shifted to the problem of invoking the Light Body into the physical body. The theory was: if the physical body's vibration could match the Light Body's vibration, the two bodies would merge.

Could the physical body's vibration be raised sufficiently? The answer was not immediately apparent.

The effort to raise the vibration of the physical body to resonate with the Light Body became the spiritual journey. The spiritual journey begins with the opening and empowerment of the base chakra and continues as each frequency of light is assimilated within physical form. Designing the human body, inventing the chakras, devoting oneself to the spiritual path, and increasing the connection with the higher-self were some of the steps taken as part of the journey to assimilate light. Vibration rose with each step, but many more steps were needed.

Invocation of the Light Body became possible once the physical body was empowered with enough light. The key was to match the Light Body's vibration. Invocation of the Light Body defines enlightenment.

Where does the spiritual journey lead to? It leads to enlightenment.

5.2 Understanding the Light Body

Understanding the Light Body starts at the top.

The divine Godhead extends into the vastness of the great void to become manifest creation. Creation enters the moments of time and the places in space. It manifests in the first moment of consciousness beyond the Godhead, then it manifests in the second moment. It manifests in the first place of consciousness beyond the Godhead, then it manifests in the second place. Creation continues to manifest in the third and fourth moments and places, then continues to extend outward into dimensions farther and farther into the void. Each level of consciousness becomes another concentric ring in the cosmic onion. The physical third dimension is the farthest level outward into which creation can still be anchored into consciousness.

The layers of consciousness immediately beyond the Godhead centre are hardly distinguishable from the Godhead. They are outside the origin, but too close to the Godhead to possess qualities that betray separation. The closest layers of creation have no identity of their own. Beyond the closest layers, separation eventually becomes apparent; and at a point far enough outside the Godhead, manifestation takes on identity.

The release of creative energy from the Godhead may be envisioned as linear projections or rays of light. God's light, then, radiates like beams of sunlight. Each beam carries one unique vibration of light outward into the ever expanding layers of consciousness beyond the Godhead. At the end of the beam, at the farthest point of consciousness from the Godhead, is the incarnate being on Earth.

The beam itself is the incarnate being's higher-self. It extends from the Godhead through every level of consciousness to Earth. Although each beam is singularly unique and complete, so too, is each level of consciousness through which it passes. Not only does the beam carry its own identity and label, each level of consciousness along the beam also carries its own identity and label. Understanding the Light Body gains momentum after sorting out the defining features used to identify and label existence[1].

Is the Light Body also the higher-self and the soul?

The higher-self is a term that distinguishes self on Earth (i.e., lower-self) from every level of self above the Earth. If the incarnate self is the lower-self, everything else is the higher-self. But the soul is

---

1 Many persons on Earth have chosen to use spiritual or angelic names to attune, not only with their own beam, but also to the multiple levels of consciousness along the beam. Using several spiritual names is not uncommon. To illustrate, as the beam of a person's higher-self radiates out from the Godhead, extending into lower and lower dimensions, and finally into the physical world, its identity and vibration change with each time and space. A spiritual or angelic name will resonate with the beam as it passes through, for example, the seventh dimension. A second spiritual or angelic name will resonate with the beam in the fourth dimension; and a third name will resonate with the dimensions of the beyond well above the eleventh dimension. In saying a particular name, its sound and vibration bring the individual into alignment with the level of consciousness from which the name arises.

not synonymous with the higher-self. The soul is the source of creative potential that wilfully projects outward from itself to manifest into the incarnate individual on Earth. Eureka! It creates you. The soul is not the higher-self; it is merely a part of the higher-self.

The soul, then, is that level of consciousness within the higher-self that created the Earthly incarnate form. None of the other levels of consciousness within the higher-self participated in the creation of the incarnate self. Therefore, none of the other levels of consciousness are properly defined as the soul.

How can the Light Body be distinguished from the higher-self?

For the individual who has not yet invoked the presence of the higher-self into the physical self, the Light Body and the higher-self are the same. The Light Body encompasses every level of consciousness emanating from the beam of the higher-self from the first level of identifiable consciousness outside the Godhead, down to the lowest level of consciousness still fully immersed within the Oneness of the lighted universe. The Light Body's defining feature is its immersion in the Oneness of the lighted universe. Again, the Light Body is the beam of being-ness from the first layer of identity down to the lowest layer still within the Oneness.

The Light Body can include the incarnate physical self!

When the incarnate physical presence on Earth becomes fully enlightened Oneness, the Light Body includes the physical presence, as well as the higher-self. The effort to fulfill the spiritual journey is merely the quest to enlighten the physical presence on Earth. Add light to the physical body and it becomes Oneness. When the physical Oneness is sufficiently enlightened, its vibration is considered to be ready to invoke the Light Body.

To be ready, the dense physical body must be prepared adequately to accommodate the extremely high and subtle frequencies of the very highest aspects of the Light Body. The effort to raise the physical body's Oneness can be quite rigorous and demanding. If the physical vibration is even marginally below the level of vibration needed to harmonize with the higher-self, the Light Body cannot be fully invoked. The Light Body will enter the physical body, but only temporarily. Its vibration is simply too fast to be compatible with the slower vibration of an inadequately prepared physical body. It separates from the physical body and returns to the heavens.

No wishful thinking involved! Either a person is ready for enlightenment, meaning that their physical vibration is high enough to resonate with every level of the higher-self, or they are not ready.

When a person is ready, the Light Body slips in quietly. The spiritual devotee is usually unaware. If the devotee anticipates cataclysmic occurrences, she will be sorely disappointed. Any euphoric imbalance within the incarnate consciousness, caused by an overwhelming rush of light entering the physical-self, occurs early in the spiritual journey. By the time a person is ready for the Light Body, the feeling of euphoria has long passed.

Because the physical vibration and the vibration of the Light Body merge at the same frequency rate, the incarnate self is unlikely to notice when the Light Body enters the physical body. Enlightenment is designed for the merging of the physical and higher-selves, and not as entertainment for the intellect's awareness. At the moment that the Light Body enters, the vibration rate of the physical body remains stable without fluctuation. The invocation of the Light Body occurs on the heels of inner peace, and so, there is no drama, euphoria, or intoxicating experience.

How will you know if you are enlightened? When Archangel Gabriel says you are, you can be sure its true. Before enlightenment, chop wood and draw water. After enlightenment, chop wood and draw water.

Because the Light Body includes every level of a being's beam of light, invocation means that the light frequencies from every level of the higher-self merge with the physical-self. Invocation has no half-measures. Either the fully unified presence of self, i.e., the entire Light Body, anchors and assimilates into the physical body, or it remains aloof.

When the definitions of soul, higher-self, and Light Body become clear, other relationships come to light. For example, awareness of the presence of the soul does not constitute Light Body invocation. During an individual's lifetime, the soul tends to check-in periodically to determine the state of the incarnate vibration, and the soul may also want to directly involve itself in the individual's growth process. If the incarnate person is aware and willing to participate, the soul can accomplish a great deal. The soul is present, but separate.

Awareness of the soul's presence can be most inspiring due to the noticeable increase in the amount of light that the soul brings. Mindful awareness of the soul, however, inherently implies separation. Union between the soul, as part of the Light Body, and the physical-self requires physical readiness. Until the physical body is ready with the appropriate level of vibration, the soul is merely "hanging around".

Understanding the Light Body can be taken further than the basics with the realization that the Light Body consists of a multitude of layers of consciousness. For the purpose of illustration, the Light Body can be subdivided: into its highest levels of consciousness, which are the first layers of identity outside the Godhead, its intermediate levels which are usually high enough to be inaccessible to Earthly consciousness, and its lowest levels which exist in the first few dimensions above the physical plane. Each level within the Light Body carries its own subtle vibration different from every other level.

Variations in the densities of the different levels of the Light Body pose differences in the way it can be accepted into the physical self. To begin, the entire Light Body remains separate from the physical self until the highest levels of the Light Body get involved. The vibration of the highest levels are too fast to be rejected or even challenged by the physical vibration. They are able to enter the physical-self without encountering resistance and easily flow in and out of the physical-self at will. The intermediate and lower levels of the Light Body, on the other hand, can only enter the physical body after the body has been reconditioned adequately. The higher the vibration of the physical body, the better it will accommodate all levels of the higher-self.

When the self at one level merges with the self at other levels, vibrational integrity must be preserved. The very highest aspect of self merges easily with the lower self without disturbing the encoded truths of God's divine plan. Intermediate levels of self, however, do not have the grace of the higher levels. They possess clearly defined identities that create separation from the lower self. Intermediate and lower-self identities may be in perfect harmony, but are too defined to permit the necessary alignment with the incarnate self. Differences in identity cannot be easily overcome. The intermediate and lower selves are subject to any form of resistance to their presence generated by the incarnate self and cannot, therefore, merge with the incarnate self at will.

In the heavenly realms, the vibrations of the higher-self readily merge with other vibrations of self, as well as the vibrations of other beings. All exists as Oneness, and Oneness can merge with any other aspect of Oneness at will. In the realm of the physical, however, self is limited. Oneness exists on the physical plane, but in relatively meagre amounts. The third-dimensional physical self cannot merge with other third-dimensional forms. Incarnate consciousness cannot enter the domain of another incarnate consciousness. For the adept master, a visit is possible, but not merged union. The vibrations of two physical beings are much too dense and tainted by negativity to accommodate the same easy flow of light through form, as happens in the heavens.

When the Light Body merges into the physical body, all levels of self vibrate in perfect alignment. The highest levels of self are already perfectly aligned. They combine with the intermediate and lower levels of self to create one unified presence—the Light Body. To complete the process, the physical self is reconditioned to vibrate at a rate that is compatible. The unified Light Body then moves to expand its presence into the Oneness of the physical body making the physical body part of the Light Body. When the physical body merges with the Oneness of the Light Body, the incarnate individual achieves enlightenment.

To redefine the Light Body after its invocation into the physical body, the Light Body is the beam of self from the first instance of identity outside the Godhead down to the physical-self on Earth including all levels of consciousness between. From top to bottom, the Light Body exists as Oneness fully connected with the lighted universe in every way.

The presence of the Light Body within the physical body, has profound implications for the acceleration of the spiritual path and evolution on Earth. Because the physical body's Oneness is consequently connected to the Oneness of the higher-self, and therefore, the Oneness of the lighted universe, the incarnate individual's access to all light frequencies in the heavens is suddenly limitless.

Prior to Light Body invocation, the connection between the physical and higher-selves depended upon an individual's wilful efforts such as prayer and meditation. If the person's wilful efforts are weak, however, so too will be her connection to her higher-self. A weak connection impedes the flow of light coming into the incarnate form. But once the Light Body has been invoked, the channel for light to flow to the physical form from the heavens opens and remains continuously open. Wilful efforts and the precarious connection with the higher-self become redundant. The physical self and higher-self are joined through Oneness; and through the Oneness, all light flows without conscious effort. Light from anywhere in the lighted universe is then potentially available to the incarnate individual.

5.3 Earth's First Light Bodies

The Light Body is contiguous with the lighted universe. In the lighted universe, the body of light is fully integrated with all creation and possesses the freedom of consciousness to move anywhere and everywhere at will. Impediments to the presence of the Light Body are non-existent. Earth, however, is not yet fully part of the lighted universe. Its often extremely dense vibration makes the presence of the Light Body difficult or even impossible. Until the empowerment of physical vibration with sufficient light, physical density prevented the descent of the Light Body.

Several millennia ago, following the concentrated efforts of legions of light-workers, the very first light bodies were invoked into the physical body. During Earth's infancy, the mass of the planet was very dimly lit. Extremely little light had arrived on Earth, and so, its vibration was too dense to accommodate any part of the multi-dimensional higher-self. A very long time might have passed before the first invocation, but light-workers soon understood the need to be innovative. Successful invocation of the Light Body followed the use of a few key innovations involving geographical light stations, etheric field manipulations, and the seven chakra system.

First, geographical light stations are places on Earth through which heavenly light flows more easily. They are highly empowered with light and have significantly raised vibration compared to their surroundings. They include centres, such as ancient Mount Shasta, places in the Himalayas, the polar regions, Ayers Rock, Sedona, Banff, Glastonbury, and others. Lamaseries, monasteries, and churches are light stations to a greater or lesser degree.

A light station possesses a vortex of light where a person can bathe in the high and subtle frequencies moving between heaven and Earth. The great masters, involved in the project to invoke the Light Body, used light stations to do their work. The richness of the available light served to awaken, empower, and prepare their Earthly bodies for the arrival of the full presence of the Light Body. Each light station was capable of drawing light frequencies from the heavens including the specialized frequencies needed to bring the physical body into alignment with the Light Body. Within the sanctity of the light station, the higher frequencies of the Light Body were given a place to come to on the physical dimension.

Second, light-workers used the Earth's etheric field to direct light onto the planet. In the beginning, the planet's etheric magnetic field was quite unstable. When the etherics vacillated, waves of light slipped through. The duration and timing of an incoming wave lasted anywhere from a few minutes to several years. The quality of the frequencies varied considerably as positive and negative vibrations crossed the etherics without scrutiny. Dark energy forces entered Earth's space, but so too did enlightened energy forces.

In using the etherics, the light-workers summoned light frequencies from the far reaches of the universe making them ready for entry onto the planet. When the etherics could be manipulated or when the appropriate vacillation occurred, watchful light-workers moved the needed frequencies into position and into physical space. Etheric manipulation was not limited to the planetary etheric field. Light frequencies had to be assimilated deep within the physical body, and so, light-workers worked also with the etheric fields of the physical body right down to the cellular level. Ultimately, light-workers used etheric manipulation to move the Light Body itself into position and into the physical body.

The more complex and higher vibrations of light that came to Earth through etheric manipulation provided the initial frequencies needed to prepare the human body. In the early experiments, each frequency was given to a select group of light-workers who then offered themselves for study. The overall objective was to bring the physical body's vibration up to a level compatible with the Light Body. As always, the process meant taking one step-at-a-time. It meant working with individual light frequencies or groups of frequencies and with individual parts of the body such as specific cells, tissues, or organs. Light-workers attempted to match light frequencies to the body parts with which the frequencies resonated. When light combined with the body's form, Oneness resulted and the body's vibration rose.

Etheric manipulation provided the means to obtain the specialized frequencies needed to prepare the physical body for invocation.

Third, until the human physical body was constructed with chakras and an internal system of delivering light to the chakras, it was unable to move enough light through its form to achieve the high vibration needed. Without chakras, light moved into the body, in a haphazard fashion. Form needed to be exposed to a stream of light that brought a greater range and quantity of frequencies to the process of assimilation. Each chakra made its own contribution in concert with each of the other chakras, and the assimilation of light into the physical body became possible. Assimilation of the specific light frequencies, which were needed to bring alignment to the physical and light bodies, then became possible.

Without the ability to move the physical and Light Bodies directly onto the physical plane together, innovation made the difference. Light stations provided a protected sanctuary. Etheric manipulation opened the way for the frequencies needed for preparation and for the Light Body to come to Earth. Finally, the chakras raised the physical body's vibration to the level needed. The light-workers, who had volunteered to work through the enlightenment process on Earth, eventually found success.

Once the first light bodies had been invoked into the physical body, light-work on Earth accelerated rapidly. Because individuals, who had achieved full enlightenment, lived on the Earth, the process of enlightenment could be understood from a third-dimensional perspective. Theories were proved or discarded. Innovations worked or were abandoned. Knowledge of the process was accumulated. With each additional invocation of the Light Body into incarnate form, more was learned and more light from the heavens found its way to Earth.

5.4 Invocation: Who and How

The invocation of the very first light-bodies took place within extremely delicate and fragile circumstances. Since those earliest of times, the process has been duplicated again and again. Earth now has an abundance of souls who have the experience of Light Body invocation.

The first successes of invocation taught light-workers how the process worked; and the experience of invocation taught the individual soul. Some souls learned well enough to help others. For the inexperienced soul, who was unfamiliar with the invocation of the Light Body on Earth, enlightenment only became possible because help was available.

Invoking the Light Body occurs within the incarnate life span. The soul extends its presence onto the physical plane to take up the incarnate form within the physical body. The physical body, however, is a temporary vehicle. When it wears out at the end of a lifetime, spirit, including the soul and Light Body, leaves the Earth to return to its potential state in the heavens. Vibration at the physical level is not carried over from one lifetime to the next. The incarnate individual must achieve the enlightened state during the current lifetime, or efforts start at the beginning with the soul's next incarnation in the next lifetime.

The opportunity to achieve enlightenment follows the same prerequisites for every incarnation. To begin, the individual must choose to be on the spiritual path of her own free-will in order to set up her physical vibration to receive light. An individual, who chooses otherwise, presents an etheric field that is either, unable to attract or assimilate appropriate frequencies, or unable to repel unwanted or harmful frequencies that then lower her vibration.

Next, during the lifetime, the physical body must assimilate an adequate quantity of light possessing the qualities needed to raise vibration. If light is in short supply or of poor quality, the body will not develop its Oneness to a vibratory state high enough to resonate with the Light Body. The path to enlightenment involves the assimilation of one frequency after another in strict sequential order. When a number of frequencies cannot be attracted, the process pauses.

Wilfully initiating the spiritual path and keeping it moving forward depends upon the strength and presence of love. Love opens the body's form to receive light, but without love, the body shifts into greater density and darkness and closes to light.

The prerequisites for Light Body invocation are the same every time: the incarnation must be willing; the physical body must be ready; and love must keep the path to enlightenment open.

A being's first attempt to achieve enlightenment quite often took a series of lifetimes. During each lifetime, the soul made a focussed effort to work with its incarnation to help create the circumstances needed for invocation. The soul acquired the skills to connect more effectively with its incarnation and to send light to the incarnate form. It evolved its understanding of how the third dimension worked. After several lifetimes, the soul learned enough to bring the physical vibration into alignment with the Light Body.

On Earth, a person has the free-will to work with the light or not to work with the light. But in the heavens, the soul also has free-will. The soul chose to be involved in the quest to bring light onto the physical plane. It agreed to be bound to the Earth until it had achieved enlightenment. By its own choice, the soul is not free to leave but is held in bondage within the galactic grid structure of our local universe, thus limiting its scope of activity to the Earth. Until it has acquired an adequate knowledge of the physical plane for the purpose of bringing the Light Body into its incarnate form, the soul remains caught in its physical experience. By achieving enlightenment, the soul's own vibration shifts enough to be free to ascend from the Earthly physical plane.

Liberation!

Because Light Body invocation liberates the soul from the physical plane, each soul incarnates into lifetime after lifetime with the goal of learning how to work with its incarnate form. The soul goes through its apprenticeship where the spiritual path becomes a familiar road. Once the soul has learned enough to invoke the Light Body, duplicating the spiritual journey gets easier. For the adept soul, knowing the process means the spiritual journey can be accomplished in the current lifetime with its own resources.

Many souls now on Earth know the process well and have achieved enlightenment many times before. Many less evolved souls, however, have yet to experience enlightenment for the first time. If the unevolved soul is unable to bring the spiritual journey to successful completion before the end of its incarnation's lifetime, help from other incarnate light-workers can make the difference.

Since the very first Light Body invocation, and in accordance with the *Pact of One*, numerous masters have chosen to incarnate for the purpose of helping others with the invocation of the Light Body. Among the many examples are the high lamas of Tibet, some of the clergy of the Catholic faith, some of the shaman and medicine men and women of the indigenous peoples, along with the high priests of ancient Egypt. For incarnate individuals who are willing, but come from an unevolved soul, help is available through the grace of a master who is encoded to facilitate Light Body invocation.

The person, who needs help, is simply unable to raise her physical vibration to an acceptable level during the span of the current lifetime. Through the grace of the empowered and enlightened master, the Light Body is offered to those whose ability falls short.

So, how does the process work?

The descent of the Light Body onto the physical plane is conducted through the connection between the soul and its incarnation. When the soul and its incarnation are unable to connect adequately, the master steps in to help. Basically, the master completes the connection and facilitates the movement of the devotee's higher-self into the physical body.

Receiving the Light Body through the grace of a master is no different than accessing the lighted universe or any other aspect of divinity. It takes love. The love, between the master and the student, is to Light Body invocation what the hockey puck is to hockey. Without it, nothing happens. Love is the most important prerequisite. Conscious effort is not required. A strong love vibration will create the circumstances and events that bring the potential candidate into the master's presence. Through love, when the student is ready, the master will come.

Love releases the seed-light of the base chakra; love empowers the chakras; love raises the body's vibration; love prepares the incarnate form-essence to receive the Light Body; love brings forth the master's help; and love opens the doorway to the heavens for the descent of the Light Body. For the truth of their love, incarnate beings cannot be denied the grace of the Light Body.

In order to acquire the Light Body through a spiritual master, the prospective candidate must project her love vibration through the master's Oneness into the highest realms of self. The master of Light Body invocation is herself enlightened without exception. As such, she is connected with every level of her own higher-self from the very highest presence of the angelic self at the first instance of identity through every dimension of consciousness down to the third dimension. Every level of her multi-dimensional higher-self is in union with every other level of self through Oneness, including physical body Oneness. Therefore, frequencies from all levels of her higher-self are able to flow through her Oneness pathways freely. In the quest to invoke the Light Body, Oneness is key.

During Light Body invocation, the unenlightened student's physical body Oneness merges, through love, with the physical body Oneness of the enlightened master. Simple physical proximity, such as being in the same room, is sufficient. Once joined in the communion of Oneness, the essence of the student moves into the master's Oneness on the physical plane. Thereafter, the student's essence ascends to the level of the highest presence of her angelic self through the Oneness of the master's unified multi-dimensional higher-self.

The connection between master and student transcends time and space and all dimensions and, therefore, also connects both of their highest levels of self. Such is the power of Oneness. The student's higher-self joins the master's higher-self. The frequencies of the master's multi-dimensional higher-self are able to flow freely through all levels of the master's Oneness down to the third dimension. Because the student's Oneness is connected to the master's Oneness, the frequencies of the student's multi-dimensional higher-self are also able to flow freely through the master's Oneness to enter the student's physical Oneness. The student's Light Body enters the physical plane and is invoked into the student's physical body through the master's Oneness.

During the invocation ceremony, because the student's Oneness uses the master's Oneness, the Light Body is protected, but dependent. Still during the invocation ceremony, the student's Light Body creates its own layers of protection and achieves independence from the master. Once the Light Body has been anchored into the physical body and exists independently, the master's role is complete.

During the remainder of the student's lifetime, the continued presence of the Light Body is maintained through the frequencies it brings into the physical body. The Light Body and the physical body share the same Oneness. Therefore, all light available to the Light Body, even at the very highest levels, is also available to the physical body. Is the physical body able to accommodate the high and subtle frequencies of the highest levels of self? Probably not, but because the Light Body is integrated and connected, it makes available the particular frequencies needed for the growth and evolution of the incarnate self, and at the time they are needed. As light can be assimilated at a much accelerated rate following enlightenment, the incarnate individual becomes highly empowered on the physical plane, further ensuring the continued presence of the Light Body.

If the enlightened individual makes life choices that lower her vibration, a problem may arise. When vibration becomes too low and dense, the physical body cannot remain in harmony with the higher-self. The higher-self is then forced to leave the physical-self. Such an occurrence is very rare and highly unlikely, but, when a person chooses without love, vibration drops. The continued presence of the higher-self (and thereby the Light Body) depends upon the continued state of the physical body's raised vibration. At the point when the presence of negativity puts the physical body's vibration below the level needed to maintain the Light Body's presence, the Light Body withdraws. Invocation will need to be done again to continue in an enlightened state.

The dawning age that is now upon us is witness to the greatest influx of light frequencies from the heavens ever. At no other time during Earth's presence on the third dimension have light frequencies arrived in greater abundance and in higher quality. More and better light is now available to empower and enlighten the Earth and its inhabitants than ever before. Because of the opportunity this moment in time affords, many beings will be experiencing enlightenment for their first time.

Along with the dramatic shift in the amount of light available is a shift in purpose for those incarnating on Earth. The mission to enlighten physical essence and the planet has not changed, but the focus has greatly intensified. Whereas in previous times, emphasis centred on the enlightenment process as an end unto itself, enlightenment has shifted to become the foundation upon which light-workers can serve higher purpose. The intent and process are unchanged, but the significantly greater amount of light now available has opened the doorway to serve higher purpose in ways that were previously beyond reach.

Because service to the light now supersedes the preoccupation with achieving enlightenment, many highly evolved beings and masters have chosen to acquire their light-bodies through the help of the graced master. Such beings are quite capable of walking their own path to enlightenment and are often more highly evolved than those empowered to invoke the Light Body. But with help, they do not need to spend the better part of a lifetime in preparation. At the appropriate moment, they connect with the master for a brief time to raise their vibration and to receive their light-bodies. They are then free to embrace the Earthly service chosen by their souls prior to incarnating and to embrace the experience of co-creation with their souls, also in service to the Earth. Enlightenment, with the help of the graced master, no longer needs to be the arduous and lengthy task it once was.

Service to the light on Earth takes numerous commonplace forms such as carpenter, artist, social worker, writer, and more. Worldly occupation does not indicate enlightenment of itself. Service comes with an individual's ability to use her place on Earth to radiate light into her surroundings. The enlightened truck driver consciously attracts light from the heavens into her own body and then project it outward as she drives along. Wherever her projection is directed, a thought-form of light energy radiates into place. Regardless of external appearances, the enlightened being can project blessings of light wherever she chooses, and light will enter into that space.

How will the spiritual devotee know who is a graced master of invocation?

The answer is found in the process itself. The first step is to express the intent to walk the spiritual path. The importance of wilful intent cannot be understated. Willingness is the first key. Thereafter, with each step on the spiritual journey, allow love to guide the way. Love is the second key. When the time is right and physical vibration is high enough, the master of invocation will appear. The body's vibration naturally attracts exactly those experiences with which it is in harmony—good or bad. Wilfully moving with love opens the doorway to Light Body invocation. The question then shifts from, "how do I find and know a graced master?" to "how can I more fully walk with love?"

Be the love and enlightenment happens. Because the moment of invocation comes with inner peace when the physical vibration and the Light Body resonate in harmony, the conscious mind may not notice. A person, who has already received the Light Body, may not be aware of its presence. After enlightenment and with no conscious effort, all that needs to unfold will unfold.

Wilfully moving with love is the key to opening the doorway to enlightenment.

Made in the USA
Charleston, SC
18 February 2012